SOCIOLOGY IN ACTION

ACTIVITIES FOR STUDENTS

Laurence A. Basirico
Elon College

 HarperCollins*CollegePublishers*

Basirico's SOCIOLOGY IN ACTION, Activities for Students

Copyright © 1993 by HarperCollins College Publishers

ISBN: 0-06-501650-5

92 93 94 95 96 9 8 7 6 5 4 3 2 1

CONTENTS

Preface

Chapter 13: *Religious Groups and Systems*

Chapter 14: *Educational Groups and Systems*   106

Chapter 15: *Political Groups and Systems*   113

Chapter 16: *Economic Groups and Systems*   120

Chapter 17: *Health Care Groups and Systems*   127

PREFACE

I have learned, from fifteen years of teaching sociology, that using the classroom as the primary teaching vehicle is too limiting. Like any discipline —scientific or artistic—sociology needs to be practiced in order to be learned. *Sociology in Action: Activities for Students* is based on the premise that students learn sociology by doing it.

This book offers a comprehensive set of assignments for students in a variety of introductory level courses such as Introduction to Sociology, Principles of Sociology, American Society, Institutions, Social Problems, and others. In addition, it is appropriate for use in introductory research methods and theory courses that are designed to introduce students to sociological inquiry.

Sociology in Action contains over three hundred introductory sociology assignments organized around over one hundred separate activity topics. There are three broad goals that these assignments are meant to accomplish: 1) to help students understand basic sociological knowledge and research; 2) to help students understand the usefulness and applications of sociological knowledge and research; and 3) to help students understand the interrelationship between basic and applied/practical sociological knowledge and research.

To accomplish these broad goals, I incorporated one or more of the following objectives into each of the activities:
1. Help students think about and understand various principles of sociology found in their text and from other sources.
2. Help students grasp and apply the major theoretical perspectives in sociology.
3. Help students make connections between the various sociological topics.
4. Challenge students to use sociological principles to enable them to think critically, interpretatively, analytically.
5. Provide students with opportunities to use cultural relativism.
6. Encourage students to think about current events using sociological knowledge.
7. Show students how to use sociological principles to understand themselves and their lives.

8. Help students obtain experience in research methods such as field work, observation, participant observation, interviewing, and library research.

9. Help students gain experience in communicating information in a variety of ways including essays, research papers, annotated bibliographies, tables, and figures.

10. Ask students to think about how sociology is useful in work settings not only for professional sociologists but for anyone who has knowledge of sociological theories, concepts, ideas, and research findings.

ORGANIZATION OF THE BOOK

Each chapter contains four to seven ACTIVITIES that focus on different themes related to the chapter's main topic. The ACTIVITIES are divided into a series of projects that include one or more of the following assignments: observation, participant observation, content analysis, interviewing, critical thinking, journal writing, essay writing, research paper writing, library research, constructing a bibliography or annotated bibliography, and making class presentations. Generally, each ACTIVITY begins with one of these assignments in which the student is asked to perform a preliminary analysis of a topic or a problem. This is usually followed by optional assignments— which may or may not be required by the professor—that ask the student to conduct further research and/or perform deeper analyses. Thus, *Sociology in Action* offers opportunities to engage students in various levels of analysis on single topics or over a broad range of topics during parts of a term or throughout the entire term.

SUGGESTIONS FOR THE PROFESSOR

There are many ways to use this book. Once you become familiar with the ways in which the ACTIVITIES are organized you will probably develop your own methods of using them in your course. Here are a few suggestions:

1. Require students to complete one (or more) of each type of assignment (for example, one journal, one essay, one research paper, one bibliography, and so on) on different topics that you choose.

2. Require students to keep a journal for the semester and complete one journal assignment (their choice or yours) for each chapter.

3. Require students to complete all of the options for one ACTIVITY, thus helping them to progress from preliminary analysis in a journal to library research to observation to a final research paper.

4. Require different students to complete different parts of an assignment and then work with each other to present a panel discussion to the class.

5. Modify the ACTIVITIES to reflect a particular concern you might have or something that you are emphasizing in class.

—Laurence A. Basirico

CHAPTER 1

The Nature and Uses of Sociology

What is the primary purpose of sociology? Is it to provide practical knowledge about how to help solve social problems (such as discrimination, racism, crime, inequality, drug abuse, poverty), help individuals or groups cope with problems (such as divorce, alcoholism, spouse abuse, and family conflicts) and help organizations make decisions (about such things as what policies they should enact, how they can operate most effectively, how to improve working conditions, and how to plan for the future)? Using sociology for these purposes is usually referred to as "applied sociology" or "sociological practice." Or is sociology's primary purpose to achieve answers to fundamental questions about the nature and processes of social life such as: why is there inequality among various groups (age, gender, race, ethnic)? How are groups organized? What is culture and how does it affect us? How do social institutions (such as the family, the economy, politics, the military, health care, religion) control our lives? Why are some individuals and groups deviant? How do we become socialized? Why does social change occur? What leads to collective behavior? Using sociology to provide fundamental knowledge about social life is usually referred to as "pure," "basic," or "academic" sociology.

While some sociologists still feel that there is a dichotomy between basic and applied sociology, many sociologists today feel that applied and basic sociology are neither mutually exclusive nor polar opposites. Sociologists are increasingly being called upon (by political and civic leaders, business leaders, news commentators, lawyers, and others) to apply theoretical models that they have developed to a real life situation.

ACTIVITY 1. 1

What Is The Purpose Of Sociology?

In *Everything in its Path* (1976), Kai Erikson writes about a disaster that occurred at Buffalo Creek, West Virginia in 1972. A mining company dam holding 132 million gallons of water burst and created a flood that devastated the community of 5,000 residents. The flood left 125 people dead and 4,000 homeless. In only a few hours, the community of Buffalo Creek was destroyed. Erikson says that he was "originally drawn to Buffalo Creek as one of several consultants to a law firm that was about to file suit on behalf of some 650 survivors" (1976, p.9). Along with lawyers, legal assistants, psychiatrists, and insurance representatives, Erikson played an instrumental part in winning $13.5 million from the coal company for the survivors.

One of Erikson's most significant discoveries was that besides the utter destruction of the physical environment of the Buffalo Creek community, the social structure was also destroyed. Erikson found that the residents of Buffalo Creek experienced individual and collective trauma. **Individual trauma** "is a blow to the psyche that breaks through one's defenses so suddenly and with such brutal force that one cannot react to it effectively... [The survivors] suffered deep shock as a result of their exposure to death and devastation, and... they withdrew into themselves, feeling numbed, afraid, vulnerable, and very alone" (Erikson, 1976, p. 153). On the other hand, **collective trauma** is "a blow to the basic tissues of social life that damages the bonds attaching people together and impairs the prevailing sense of communality" (p. 154). The people began to realize that they could no longer depend upon each other for any kind of support and that each was wholly dependent on their own individual resources. "'I' continue to exist. . 'You' continue to exist ... But 'we' no longer exist as a connected pair or as linked cells in a larger communal body" (p. 154).

Journal instructions :
1. Think of a natural or human-made disaster that occurred near you that caused massive destruction to a community within the last ten years: tornado, hurricane, earthquake, flood, mud slide, urban rioting, environmental contamination, or others.

2. Locate and read ten newspaper or magazine articles that described the event. Be sure your articles cover a period of at least two to three weeks.

3. In your journal, keep a record of the information (data) reported in each article. Look for two types of data: quantitative and qualitative. **Quantitative** data are the numerical "facts" (for example, how many victims, how much damage, and so on). The **qualitative** data are the written or spoken

"comments" (feelings, interpretations, ideas, and so on) made by observers (victims, journalists, public officials, and so on). What was the main focus (quantitative or qualitative data) of the news articles during the first day or two after the event?

4. How did the focus of the articles change after about a week? After two or three weeks? How did the types of quantitative and qualitative data reported about in the article change?

5. If possible, interview someone who experienced the event. Ask the person what it was like when the event was occuring, what it was like for them right after it occured, and what it was like a few weeks later. If it is not possible for you to interview someone who experienced the event, try to obtain this information from interviews that were conducted by news reporters and journalists.

6. From what you learned about the event you researched, what can you say about how natural or human-made disasters affect individuals and society?

7. How might the information you obtained from your research be useful to people in the following occupations: insurance adjusters, lawyers, clergy, politicians? Are there any other occupations in which you think the information you found might be useful?

8. What do you think is most important from what you have learned from your research about this event: knowledge about how disasters affect people in general, or knowledge that can be used to help the people who experienced that particular event? Why?

Option: essay
Write an essay (around four to five pages, typed) in which you use your journal answers (above) to discuss the applied (practical) and basic uses of sociology.

Option: class presentation
Prepare a five- to ten-minute presentation to your class about the data and comments you discussed in your journal.

ACTIVITY 1. 2

Should Personal Values Enter Into Scientific Research?

An important consideration about the use of sociology is whether or not sociologists should allow their values - personal, political, social, moral - to influence their research. In 1918, the classic social theorist Max Weber suggested that sociology, like other sciences, should be "value-free." That is, Weber felt that scientists should strive to find out the "facts," and leave their personal views out of their work (Babbie, 1992, p. 476). Many social scientists since Weber agree that the goal of scientific research should be the discovery and development of knowledge in and of itself.

Other sociologists, such as Alvin Gouldner (1962), feel that social scientists have a responsibility to use their knowledge to follow their personal, social, and political consciences. Still others, such as Howard Becker (1967), believe that it is impossible for sociologists to leave their values out of their work. Rather, Becker feels that they must recognize the impossibility of doing "value-free" science and decide what position they will advocate.

Journal instructions:
1. Interview four faculty members (from your school and/or elsewhere) about whether or not personal, social, political, and moral values should play a part in the research in their discipline. Interview two faculty members from social science departments (sociology, anthropology, history, political science, economics) and two from natural science departments (biology, chemistry, physics). Record your interviews in your journal. Use the following questions as a guide, and develop additional questions if you wish:
   a) Are there any types of research that you think scientists in your discipline should not undertake?
   b) Are there any conditions in which scientists should not report the results of their research?
   c) Suppose you were asked to testify in court (either as a paid "expert witness" or as a result of a subpoena) in a discrimination case and you knew that the results of your research could be used by an attorney in an argument to justify a type of discrimination of which you disapprove. What would you do?
   d) Would you conduct groundbreaking research in your field that, in the opinion of your colleagues, was going to make a considerable contribution to solving a problem in your discipline, yet likely would be used to benefit some groups at the expense of others?
   e) If you were asked by the government to join a team of scientists to assess the physical and social consequences of a particular type of warfare, what would you do?

Option: essay
Using the data you collected in your journal, write an essay (around three to four pages, typed) in which you discuss whether there are differences or similarities in how social scientists and natural scientists view the issue of "value-free" science.

ACTIVITY 1.3

An Introduction to Sociological Journals

This activity is designed to introduce you to library research in sociology, to familiarize you with a few of the major sociological journals, to give you some practice in documenting sociological sources, to provide you with a sense of the types of research that sociologists conduct, to help you see the connections and distinctions between basic and applied sociology, and to help you see how values might enter into research.

Instructions:
1. Locate the section of your library that houses the sociology journals. Become familiar with how to access current and back issues. Ask your librarian for help.

2. Select five titles of sociology research journals that your library subscribes to (for example, *The American Journal of Sociology*, *American Sociological Review*, *Social Forces*, and many others). You may want to ask your professor to recommend which journals to look for. For the purposes of this assignment, do not use journals of book reviews (such as *Contemporary Sociology*) or journals that focus only on teaching (such as *Teaching Sociology*). For each journal:
   a) Obtain one issue for each journal title you selected. Thus, you will have five journal issues.
   b) Go through each issue and pick out three or four articles that you think might be interesting. (Pick only articles, not review essays, editorials, or book reviews.) Provide complete bibliographic information for each article you selected (author, title, journal, volume, date, pages). You should wind up with around fifteen to twenty articles.
   c) Without reading the articles you select (read only the title and the abstract), write down what you think the purpose of the research described in the article is oriented more toward: basic sociology or applied sociology, or both. What makes you think this?
   d) From the title of the article and the abstract only, discuss how a sociologist's values might influence the choice of the research topic, how the study might be conducted, and how the results might be presented?

3. Present your material in the form of an **annotated bibliography**. An annotated bibliography is a bibliography that contains a brief comment after each book or article listed. In your annotated bibliography for this activity, make your comments with regard to "c" and "d" (above). See the examples on the next page and look at the way the references are listed in some of the journals that you selected.

Example of reference format used in most sociology journals:
Becker, Howard S. 1967. "Whose Side Are We On?" *Social Problems* 14: 239-247.

Gergen, Kenneth J. 1991. *The Saturated Self: Dilemmas of Identity in Contemporary Life.* New York: Basic Books.

Example of annotated bibliography:
Becker, Howard S. 1967. "Whose Side Are We On?" *Social Problems* 14: 239-247.
Becker argues that it is neither possible nor desirable for sociologists to take a value-free position in their work. Instead, he says, they should ascertain the position that they intentionally or unintentionally advocate.

Gergen, Kenneth J. 1991. *The Saturated Self: Dilemmas of Identity in Contemporary Life.* New York: Basic Books.
This is a fascinating exploration of how shifts in perspectives from romanticism to modernism to post-modernism have affected science, art, literature, music, and ultimately, the conceptions we have of ourselves. It provides excellent insight into the impact of theoretical perspectives on what is perceived as real.

ACTIVITY 1. 4

How Is Sociology Used At Work?

Students, parents, and college placement counselors often misunderstand and underestimate the types of jobs for which sociology can help prepare you. A common misperception is that the only type of employment that undergraduate sociology prepares you for is social work or other social service-oriented occupations. This is not true. In fact, if you wish to become a professional social worker, it would probably be better for you to obtain your B.A. or B.S. degree (and probably an M.A. or M.S. degree) in social work or human services than in sociology. Another misperception is that people with graduate degrees in sociology (master's or Ph.D) only become college professors. While it is true that a person usually has to have a Ph.D in sociology to become an academic sociologist, people with a doctoral or a master's degree are employed in many different ways. They work as city planners, researchers for private and public organizations (such as insurance companies, banks, service organizations, and so on), counselors and therapists, advertisers, and many other areas. A third misperception is that only people with graduate degrees can use their sociological knowledge to help them in their work. Wrong again. Sociological knowledge and skills are used in most jobs.

6

Journal instructions:
1. Interview people from five different types of careers. Try to get a wide variety: health care professionals (physicians, nurses, physical therapists, and so on), business executives, advertisers, architects, engineers, government workers, insurance agents, bankers, counselors, consultants, and so on. You do not have to limit yourself to these suggestions. Ask each person the following questions in regard to their work. If they answer yes, ask them to please explain. Record your interviews in your journal.

  a) Do you ever need to know about the behavior and lifestyle of people from different age, income, racial, or ethnic groups?

  b) Do you ever need to understand the similarities and differences between males and females?

  c) Do you ever need to understand about how people learn (to follow instructions, to communicate with others, to become a member of a group, and so on)?

  d) Do you ever need to understand how and why people interact with each other?

  e) Do you ever need to understand why conflict or harmony occurs in particular situations?

  f) Do you ever need to understand why different social trends occur (such as fads and fashions) and how to predict how long they might last?

  g) Do you ever need to know how to create situations that might help people become more effective in their work?

  h) Do you ever need to know how to evaluate whether or not your organization is meeting its goals?

  i) Do you ever need to know how to assess what the needs of your clientele are and how you might make changes in your work to better meet those needs?

  j) Do you ever need to understand how different social trends are going to affect people's behavior?

  k) Do you ever need to do any type of research or conduct a survey?

  l) Do you ever need to understand why people fail to obey rules or laws?

2. After each interview, carefully look through the detailed table of contents in your introductory sociology text. (If your book does not have a detailed table of contents, look through the headings within each chapter of the book.) Make a list of the topics found within each chapter that could provide helpful information in the careers of each of the people you interviewed.

Option: class presentation
Complete the above journal instructions. Then, using your journal as your source of information, prepare a five- to ten-minute class presentation about the ways in which sociology could be useful in particular occupations.

CHAPTER 2

The Development of Sociology

Auguste Comte and Emile Durkheim, two of the earliest social theorists, believed that there are social facts or truths that exist independently of individuals. That is, there is objective social knowledge outside of us to be discovered. Just as astronomers use telescopes to study the galaxies and biologists use microscopes to study cells, the first sociologists maintained that objective knowledge of the social world could be obtained by observing and measuring different aspects of human behavior: income, gender, education, race, crime, divorce, suicide, religion, politics, and many others.

However, Max Weber, another classic social theorist, believed that it is not enough to examine the social facts to understand social reality. Weber felt that we must try to understand social reality in terms of those who are experiencing it. Besides using objective methods to observe social life, sociologists must develop ways to understand the subjective, personal meanings that people attach to their own behavior and to the behavior of others. The *verstehen* approach, as Weber called it, calls for sociologists to immerse themselves into the living experience of those whom they are researching.

To illustrate the difference between observing social facts and the verstehen approach, consider the different ways that the American family could be studied. Sociologists observing social facts about the family might collect data about different types of family structures, role relationships within families, the functions of families, interaction patterns, family conflict, marriage rates, divorce rates, birth rates, and so on. Sociologists guided by the *verstehen* approach might be interested in finding out what the experience of family means to different family members, how family members come to construct and share a reality, how members in a particular family come to experience and interpret the outside world, what it means to experience a divorce, and so on (Hewitt, 1988).

8

There are numerous sociological theories and perspectives that are rooted in both of these approaches. Most contemporary sociologists do not adhere to only one, but realize that there are a variety of methods and perspectives that must be used to understand the social world.

ACTIVITY 2. 1

Understanding Social Reality: Facts Or Interpretations?

This activity should help to give you a good idea about the relative merits and difficulties of obtaining "objective" and "subjective" knowledge of a social situation.

Journal instructions:
1. Select a social situation that you have never experienced, know very little about, or at least have never observed in a systematic way and observe it for three hours (for example, a nursing home, an abortion clinic, a particular sporting event, a hospital emergency room, a gay bar, an auction, and so on). Keep a journal in which you record only the objective facts you observe. For example, how many people are there, what do they look like (dress, sex, race, and so on), what are they doing, what is the setting like, and anything else that you can determine by using your physical senses alone. Take extensive notes. Write down as many details as you can.

2. Observe the same situation for another three hours. This time, do not record the objective facts. Instead, keep a written record of what you think the people in the situation are thinking and feeling. As you do this, explain what leads you to make these interpretations.

Option: essay
Use the data (information) you collected from the above and write an essay (four to five pages, typed) in which you fully describe and discuss the nature of the social situation that you observed. Develop some conclusions about the social situation you observed and then try to make some generalizations or predictions about similar types of social situations. (For example, if you observed rock musicians, what might you predict about other types of entertainers? If you observed nursing-home residents, what might you predict about people in other confined settings, such as prison? If you observed spectators at a sporting event, what might you predict about other types of situations where there are large crowds?) Include a discussion about the methods you used to discover what was "really" going on in the situation you observed:
   a) Which types of observations (the objective facts or interpretations of what people were thinking and feeling) did you find were the most helpful

in arriving at your conclusions about the group and in making your generalizations?

b) Is it possible to observe and record just the objective facts of a situation without making some type of interpretation?

c) Is it possible to make interpretations about what people are thinking and feeling without also considering what the objective facts of the situation are?

ACTIVITY 2. 2

How Do Theoretical Perspectives Influence The Way Sociologists See?

A theoretical perspective in sociology is a model or a framework that organizes the way we look at social life. The particular theoretical perspective that we use influences what we study, the questions we ask, the explanations we arrive at, and the types of solutions we pose. While sociology has many such theoretical perspectives, the dominant ones are structural functional theory, conflict theory, and symbolic interaction theory.

Structural functional theory focuses on the parts - for example, societies or groups - of a social system, tries to determine what each part does, and explains how the parts are related to each other. From this perspective, social life is viewed as one of cooperation and consensus among the various parts of a system with basic agreements about its goals, values, and beliefs, thus creating a system which runs smoothly.

Conflict theory sees social life as a struggle between groups and individuals for scarce resources. From this view, social systems are characterized by conflict and competition between those who are dominant and those who are subordinate, with social arrangements that generally benefit the dominant groups.

Symbolic interaction theory views social life as a process of individuals interacting. From this perspective, people interact through a series of symbols, including language and gestures, having learned what different symbols mean as a result of being socialized into a culture, society, or group.

Go to your introductory sociology textbook, study these theories, and make sure you have a solid understanding of them before proceeding with this activity.

Journal instructions:
1. Select an organized group (for example, a fraternity or sorority, sports team, club, committee, employees, and so on) in which you are a new member (about a month or less). If you are not currently a new member of a group,

select a group that interests you and that you have access to observing. Record the following in your journal:

a) Develop a list of questions that each of the above theoretical perspectives —structural functional theory, conflict theory, and symbolic interaction theory—might try to answer about the group you choose to observe.

b) What preconceptions would each of the above theoretical perspectives lead you to have about the particular group you choose, before actually observing the group?

c) Observe the group for one hour on three separate occasions and record your observations in rich detail. On the first occasion, take great care to observe the group as if structural functional theory offers the only possible explanations of social life. On the second occasion, observe the group as if conflict theory offers the only possible explanations. On the third occasion, observe the group as if symbolic interaction theory offers the only possible explanations. Again, record your observations in rich detail and exercise great care to look from only one perspective on each occasion.

2. After you have completed your observations, use them to answer the following question in your journal:

a) Which of your initial preconceptions of the group tended to be the most true?

b) Which of the theoretical perspectives do you think provided the most useful model for explaining the "true" nature of the group?

c) Did you have any difficulty observing the group on each occasion using only one perspective? If so, explain.

Option: essay
Use the journal (above) to write an essay (around five pages, typed) in which you analyze the group you selected from structural functional, conflict, and symbolic interactionist perspectives.

ACTIVITY 2. 3

How A Classic Social Theorist Might View Your World

Theoretical perspectives influence the way we interpret social events. This activity should help you understand the way this occurs. Be creative with this activity. Besides being fun, it should give you a good understanding of the views of some classic social theorists.

Journal instructions:
1. Select three classic social theorists that are discussed in your introductory sociology text. Reread the sections in your text on each of these theorists very carefully.

2. Borrow a textbook on sociological theory from your library, from one of the sociology professors at your school, or from a student who has taken a course in sociological theory. There are many good texts available (for example, Ashley and Orenstein, 1990; Collins, 1985; Collins and Makowsky, 1988; Coser, 1977; Ritzer, 1988; Turner, 1986; and many others). Read the chapters about the theorists you selected and take notes about their lives, the type of society in which they lived (for example, the economic and political climate), their ideas, and the theories they developed.

3. Make a list in your journal of things that each of these three theorists might be interested in looking at and explaining if they were living your life today. For example, Karl Marx would probably pay particular attention to the ways in which people try to maintain their dominance in various situations and the types of conflict that occur in various aspects of social life. Emile Durkheim would probably pay particular attention to the ways in which group solidarity is created and the collective ways in which people come to interpret things. These are only a few examples. There are innumerable others. Make as extensive a list as you can for each theorist. Be creative.

4. Spend one day as each theorist thinking about how that theorist might live your life today (total of three days). Use the list you developed above for ideas of what to observe. For each day (that is, for each theorist), keep an extensive journal of your observations and interpretations of the world around you as if you were that theorist. In your journal, include discussions of conversations you have with others (speaking with them from the point of view of the theorist), interpretations and reactions to the news, interpretations and reactions to everyday events in your life, reactions of others to your (that is, the theorist's) views, and so on.

Option: essay
After you have completed your three day journal, write a paper (around three to five pages, typed) in which you compare how each of the three theorists would act and think if they were living your life. In your paper, be sure to explain what events or situations that you encounter would be of particular interest to each theorist, what they might think about it, and why.

ACTIVITY 2.4

**Using Theoretical Perspectives To Explore
Controversial Social and Political Issues**

As you have read in your introductory sociology text, sociology offers insights that go beyond common sense. Some of these insights can be very useful for examining controversial social and political issues. One very controversial persistent social and political issue is whether or not abortion should remain legal. In 1973, the U.S. Supreme Court decided in Roe v. Wade to allow women to have an abortion when there is little risk to their health or before the fetus is able to survive outside the womb. However, the abortion issue was not settled once and for all with that decision. As you know, debate over whether or not abortion should be legal continues to this day and was a major issue in the 1992 presidential election. It is not likely that the controversy will ever be settled once and for all. The battle between "pro-choice" and "pro-life" advocates (political and civic leaders, religious leaders, members of activist groups, and so on) has become, at times, intense and emotionally charged. When an issue becomes emotionally charged, people often have a difficult time examining it from any perspective other than their own. This activity asks you to put your personal and emotional views aside and to look at the various sides of the abortion debate.

Journal instructions:
1. Interview three "pro-life" and three "pro-choice" advocates on your campus or in your community. For each, find out their gender, race, highest level of education, religion, occupation, marital status, age and (if possible) income level. Ask them the following questions and record the responses in your journal:
   a) Why do you feel abortion should be illegal or legal?
   b) What do you feel are the major considerations in the debate over legalized abortion?
   c) Why do you think the debate is so controversial and why does it persist?
   d) What are your views about pre-marital sex?
   e) Do you feel that sex is primarily for procreation or for pleasure?
   f) Do you feel that women should be equal to men in rights and responsibilities in the family?
   g) Do you feel that women should have the same employment opportunities as men?
   h) Who do you think should be primarily responsible for taking care of the children in a family: mother, father, both?

2. In your journal, analyze the responses to the questions from the point of view of each of the major theoretical perspectives in sociology. How would each explain what the controversy is really about and why it exists?

Option: research paper
1. In the library find four articles listed in the *Reader's Guide to Periodical Literature* and four articles listed in the *Social Science Index* within the last year that contain debates or discussions about the abortion controversy. Read the articles and outline the reasons they provide for and/or against keeping abortion legal. Be sure to find enough articles that provide you with arguments for and against legalized abortion.

2. Using the information from your journal and library research, write a paper (around five to seven pages, typed) in which your present well-organized arguments for keeping abortion legal and for making abortion illegal. Use the theoretical perspectives in sociology as a framework to organize the data that you have collected and to develop your positions for and against legalized abortion. Be sure to leave your personal feelings and emotions out of the positions for and against legalized abortion, and provided a balanced debate. Provide proper documentation of your references throughout your paper and include a reference (works cited) page.

ACTIVITY 2. 5

**How Mental Health Researchers and Therapists
Are Guided by Theoretical Perspectives**

Although many people are guided by theoretical perspectives in their work, this is especially true for people who work in disciplines related to mental health. Whether one has a degree in sociology, psychology, human services, or social work, people who work in the field of mental health - therapists, researchers, directors of organizations, and others - usually rely on one or more theories to guide their work.

Journal instructions:
Interview a mental health worker—either a therapist, a researcher, or a director of a mental health organization. If possible, interview a mental health worker with a graduate degree in sociology. If you cannot find a sociologist in a mental health profession, see if one of the faculty in your sociology department has knowledge in the area of mental health. A third option, if neither of the above two is available, is to interview someone with a graduate degree in psychology, human services, or social work. Ask the person:
a) What theoretical perspectives or theories guide you or are important in your work?
b) Could you give an example of how you use theories or theoretical perspectives in your work?
c) Are there any alternative theories or perspectives to the ones you use? If so, how would the way you do your work be different if you used them?

CHAPTER 3

Methods of Studying Society

Sociology is a science. People often mistakenly use the word "science" synonymously with "natural science." The social sciences—sociology, anthropology, political science, psychology, economics, history—and the natural sciences —biology, physics, chemistry—are sciences because of how they obtain and develop their knowledge. A body of knowledge is considered to be a branch of science because it is derived from using scientific method, not because of its specific subject matter. Although the natural and social sciences have different techniques relative to their respective subject matter, they each rely on various methods of systematic observation and analysis - the basic principles of the scientific method.

Another misconception that some people have is that research is something only scientists do. While not everyone needs to use all of the sophisticated techniques that social and natural scientists use, some form of systematic research is important and necessary in many areas of our personal lives and in almost every occupation.

ACTIVITY 3. 1

Using The Library For Research

Although most sociological research uses some form of observation, it generally starts in the library. You may need background information, facts, current data, expert opinions, public opinion, sociological or other scientific articles, or other important information necessary to conduct your research. Or you may be using the results of other people's research to write your own paper. No doubt, most of you are familiar with how to use a library's card catalogue or on-line computer catalogue for locating books. However, there are numerous other library research materials that might offer you more appropriate or more current information. These include reference books, indexes, abstracts, professional journals, government documents, newspapers, magazines, and many other research materials and services that your library offers. The key to beginning any sociological library research is knowing which research materials are appropriate for your work, how to access them, and how to use them.

While there are innumerable research materials and services that libraries offer - some libraries have more than others - the following are a few essential ones to get you started with sociological research. Most college libraries will have these and many others:

- *Reader's Guide to Periodical Literature.* This index, published semi-monthly from September to June and monthly in July and August, provides lists of articles, organized by topic, that have appeared recently in popular, news, and commentary magazines (for example, *Time, Newsweek, New Perspectives Quarterly, New Republic, The Nation, Harper's, National Review,* and many others).

- *Social Science Index.* This will probably be the most useful source of articles for you and the best place to start. This index, published four times a year, contains a detailed list of articles that have appeared recently in scholarly social science journals. Most libraries contain a variety of other generalized and specialized indexes (for example, *Social Sciences Citation Index, Education Index)* that may suit your needs.

- *Contemporary Sociology.* Published six times a year by the American Sociological Association, this is a journal of reviews and essays about current books in sociology. It has a table of contents organized by sociological topic and is an excellent source for finding out about the latest books in each area.

- *Sociological Abstracts.* An abstract is a brief summary that usually appears at the beginning of a journal article. The *Sociological Abstracts*, published six times a year, is a collection of all of the abstracts that have appeared in most of the professional sociological journals recently. There are *abstracts* for many other scholarly disciplines as well (such as *Psychological Abstracts)* that your library may have.

- *U.S. Bureau of the Census Statistical Abstract of the United States.* Published annually, this is a national data book and guide to sources. Includes vital state and national statistics on population, immigration, education, crime, marriage, divorce, and so on. There are many other government and non-government documents that can also provide you with current statistics.

- Inter-library loan. Your library probably has an inter-library loan service. If your library does not have the specific research material you need (journal, book, reference, and so on), they will be able to obtain it for you within a week or so from another library. By taking advantage of this service, any college library can grant you access to virtually any research material that you may need.

There are research materials (such as specialty indexes, abstracts, sources of government and non-government data, computer indexes, and so on) that could be useful for your specific research. Once you become familiar with the above materials, you will have no trouble locating and using others.

Bibliography instructions:
1. Familiarize yourself with the above research materials.
   a) Ask your reference librarian which of the above (and which additional research materials) your library has.
   b) Find out where the above research materials are located in your library.
   c) Become familiar with how to use each of them. Instructions are usually provided in the beginning of each item. If you need help, ask your reference librarian.

2. Select **one** of the following topics:
   a) Income inequality in the United States.
   b) The extent of the AIDS crisis in the U.S. and in the world.
   c) The health care crisis in America.
   d) The successes and failures of the American education system.

3. Using the research materials listed above, compile an extensive bibliography (around twenty sources) that would provide you with the information necessary to discuss and analyze the topic you selected. Use the bibliography (list of references) from one of the articles as a model to follow. (Also, see Activity 1. 3.) Make sure your bibliography contains sources that could provide you with the following:
   a) contrasting opinions about the extent of the problem and about how it might be solved
   b) quantitative data (numerical facts about current trends)
   c) current sociological research about the topic

4. Find out which items in your bibliography are available in your library. Make a notation next to the items on your bibliography that your library has.

5. For the items on your bibliography that are not available in your library, ask your reference librarian which ones are available through inter-library loan. Make a notation next to the items on your bibliography that your library can get through inter-library loan.

Option: journal
1. In your journal, make a list of four or five occupations (for example, health care, counseling, consulting, education, journalism, law, insurance, business, and many others) that could use the information provided by the items in your bibliography. If you cannot think of any, discuss this with a career counselor at your school. For each occupation you list, briefly indicate (a sentence or two) how the information provided by the items in your bibliography might be used.

2. Interview two people who work in any of the occupations you identified and ask them about the types of research that they use, refer to, or need to conduct in their work. Show them the bibliography you compiled and ask them for reactions to it. Is it relevant to their work? Is it useful? Do they use similar types of research material when they are trying to solve problems within their job? And so on. Record your the responses to your interviews in your journal.

ACTIVITY 3. 2

Using Sociological Research In Your Work

Knowledge that is based on current sociological research is useful in many types of occupations and careers. It would be difficult to think of an occupation that does not, at times, have problems or face an issue that is sociologically related. If you know how to access the most current sociological studies and critically analyze them, you may be able to help solve some of these problems and improve your effectiveness in your occupation.

Bibliography instructions:
Below is a list of occupations and specific problems that someone employed in that occupation might need to address. For each item, find a research article (that is, an article based on research, not simply an essay or review) that appears in a recent sociology (or other social science) journal. Include the author, name of the article, journal, date, and the pages on which the article appears. Use the bibliography (list of references) from one of the articles as a model to follow. (Also, see Activity 1. 3.)

(Hint: You do not have to locate articles that address the specific occupations. Rather, focus on the need or problem that is addressed by each.)

1. a therapist who wants to know more about how alcoholism affects families
2. a journalist who wants to understand more about the extent and causes of racism in inner cities

3. a physician who wants to obtain objective insights about the nature of the health care crisis in America

4. a politician who wants to understand about the savings and loan crisis

5. a law enforcement officer who wants to understand how to control large crowds

6. a city planner who wants to determine how much money should be budgeted for helping the elderly

7. a school administrator who wants to know more about the extent of sexism in schools

8. a human resource consultant who wants to know more about how to create a work environment that addresses the needs of minorities

9. a lawyer who wants to understand the different types of discrimination and why they occur

10. a clergy person who wants to counsel families of AIDS victims

11. an elementary school teacher who wants to understand differences in learning between males and females

12. an insurance agent who wants to understand about the changing lifestyles of the elderly and how it might affect their insurance needs

Option: journal

1 Select one of the above problems and locate the accompanying article that you identified.

2. In your journal, discuss what the article is about, the research methods the author(s) used, and how it might be useful in providing some insights into the occupational problem you selected. To guide you in your journal discussion, address the following items about the research article. (Go to your introductory sociology text for a definition of each of the items listed below):

   a) Discuss the purpose of the research (descriptive, explanatory, evaluative, or something else).

   b) Identify the important concepts, theories, and variables (dependent and independent).

   c) Discuss how the variables are operationally defined. That is, how does the researcher define the variables in such a way that they can be measured?

   d) What is the population that the research attempts to generalize about?

   e) Is there a sample of the population that the researcher used? If so, what type of sample (random, representative, and so on) was it and how was it selected?

   f) Identify and discuss the methods that the researcher used (observation, survey research, experiments, and so on).

   g) Discuss how the research article might be useful in addressing the problem you selected above.

ACTIVITY 3. 3

Designing A Research Project

Besides conducting library research, you may need to design your own research project to help you solve a problem. See the chapter on research methods in your sociology text for a definition of the items listed in this activity.

Journal instructions:
1. Think of an occupation in which you think you might work some day.

2. Think of a problem that you might face in that occupation that is sociologically related. (For examples, see Activity 3.2, above).

3. In your journal, design a research project that could provide information that might help you solve or deal with the problem. Address the following items:
   a) What is the purpose of the research: descriptive, explanatory, evaluative, other?
   b) What sociological theories or concepts might be useful in helping you think about the problem?
   c) What would the independent and dependent variables be?
   d) How could you operationally define the variables?
   e) What is the population you would want to generalize about?
   f) Would you use a sample? If so, what type, and how would you select it?
   g) Discuss which methods you would use to carry out the research (survey, observation, participant observation, experiment, and so on.
   h) How would the results of your project help you to solve or deal with the problem that you designed the research about?

Option: essay
Use the above information that you compiled in your journal to write a research proposal—that is, an essay which describes the project you are proposing (around five pages, typed) - in which you discuss the research methods for carrying out such a project.

ACTIVITY 3. 4

Ethics in Social Research

Social scientists generally agree that there are a number of ethical principles that must be adhered to when doing research that involves human subjects. Subjects must not be harmed (physically, psychologically, emotionally, or otherwise), they must agree to participate voluntarily and be well-informed about the experiment and any risks, and their privacy must be protected. Scientists are also concerned about the ways in which the results of the research are reported and how they will be used. (For thorough discussions of these ideas, see the texts listed in the suggested readings and the bibliographies contained within those texts).

The following are examples of studies that are notorious for containing ethical problems:

Milgram, Stanley. 1963. "Behavioral Study of Obedience." Journal of Abnormal and Social Psychology 67: 371-378.

Humphreys, Laud. 1970. *Tearoom Trade: Impersonal Sex in Public Places*. Chicago: Aldine.

Reiss, Albert. 1968. "Police Brutality: Answers to Key Questions." *Transaction* 5: 10-19.

Haney, C., Banks, W. C., and Zimbardo, P. 1973. "Interpersonal Dynamics in a Simulated Prison." *International Journal of Criminology and Penology* 1: 69-97. (This is more commonly referred to as Zimbardo's study.)

Journal instructions:
Locate and read three of the above studies, or read discussions about them that appear elsewhere. Many research methods and introductory textbooks contain discussions of them (for example, Eshleman et al (1993); Babbie (1992); Frankfort-Nachmias and Nachmias (1992); Singleton (1988); Smith (1991); and many others). Then, in your journal, discuss the following:
a) What was the purpose of the study? (That is, what was the researcher trying to find our or accomplish?)
b) Briefly summarize the research methods used in the study. (That is, what did the researcher do to try to find out what he/ she wanted to?)
c) Discuss the ethical dilemmas involved in the research.
d) Could the research have been conducted in a way that these ethical dilemmas could have been avoided, yet still obtain the knowledge that the researcher was after? How?

Option: essay
Based upon your above journal work, write an essay (around five pages, typed) in which you summarize the types of ethical problems that can occur in social science research, and illustrate them with examples taken from specific sociological research. You can use the ones you discussed in your journal and/or others.

ACTIVITY 3. 5

Discovering Ethical Problems in Research

Sometimes, the ethical problems that exist in a research project are not obvious. This may be because the researcher recognized what they might be and took great pains to overcome them. Or it might be that the researcher did not recognize any ethical problems because they were unanticipated or too subtle to see. In any event, it is important that you become sensitive to the types of ethical problems that exist in research that is already completed or research that you might be doing yourself.

Instructions:
1. Locate a sociology journal article on one of the following topics:
   a) illegal drug users
   b) sexual behavior
   c) voting attitudes
   d) behavior of college students
   e) AIDS victims

2. Write an essay (around four to five pages, typed) in which you address the following:
   a) What is the objective of the research described in each article?
   b) What types of ethical considerations do you think the researcher considered, or should have considered, when designing the project?
   c) Describe the research method used in each of the studies.
   d) In the methods used in each study, what did the researcher do to overcome any possible ethical difficulties?
   e) As far as you can tell, are there any ethical problems with how the research was conducted or how it was reported that the researcher overlooked? If so, how could you eliminate these ethical problems if you were doing the research?

CHAPTER 4

Culture and Society

A **culture** is a system of ideas, values, beliefs, knowledge, norms, symbols, language, customs, and technology shared by almost everyone in a particular society. Simply, culture is the shared reality of people in a society. A **society** is a group of interacting people who live in a specific geographical area, who are organized in a cooperative manner, and who share a common culture. Thus, people within a particular society have similar ways of perceiving the world around them and acting within it.

The world consists of thousands of different cultures and subcultures. Hence, there are hundreds of ways of perceiving the world and acting within it. However, people from different cultures are not isolated from each other. On the contrary, we live in a world which increasingly brings us into contact with people from cultures other than the predominant culture within which we live. There are many reasons for this. For example:

• The number of Hispanic, African, and Asian Americans is increasing. (If current trends in immigration and birth rates continue, half of the United States population will be nonwhite by 2020.)
• Multinational corporations are proliferating. (Many companies and corporations are no longer confined to one country, but have production facilities in many countries. American and Japanese automobile companies are prime examples).
• The Iron Curtain and Soviet Communism have been dismantled. (For decades, many Eastern Europeans were unable to leave their country. The borders of Eastern European countries are now permeable, allowing members of many different countries to migrate elsewhere.)
• Advances in travel and communications technology increasingly enables people from different cultures to interact easily. (Fax machines, computer networks, high-speed air travel, and other technological achievements enable us to communicate with people in different countries in a very short period of time.)

Considering the various cultures with which you are likely to come into contact, it is important to understand the impact that culture has on people and to be able to recognize the validity of cultures other than our own.

ACTIVITY 4. 1

Culture And The Self

Journal instructions:
1. Re-read the section in your textbook that discusses the elements or components of culture (norms, values, beliefs, symbols, language, artifacts, and technology).

2. Write down each element or component of culture at the top of a separate page in your journal, one per page, and define it in your own words. (That is, write down "norm" at the top of a page and define it, "values" at the top of another page and define it, and so forth). Allow two or three pages of blank space for each.

3. Keep your journal with you at **all times** for three days. Four or five times each day, spend about fifteen minutes briefly writing about examples of the elements or components of culture that have affected you that day or at that moment. The following are some questions that might help you organize your ideas:
   a)   What element(s) of your dominant culture affected you or did you experience (for example, norm, value, symbol, and so on) during a particular situation?
   b)   Describe the specific example. For example, if it was a norm, what was it?
   c)   Briefly describe the situation in which the cultural element (that is, the norm, value, symbol, and so on) affected you. That is, where were you and what were you doing at the time?
   d)   Briefly discuss why or how you think that particular cultural element (that is, the particular norm, value, and so on) developed. This may require some speculation on your part.
   e)   What social function or purpose does it serve?
   f)   How important is it that you follow it?
   g)   What happens if you do not follow it?
   h)   In general, how do you feel about this particular cultural element?

4. After keeping your journal for three days, read it over and develop a list of categories or types of situations that you could use to summarize your comments. Some examples of categories might be family situations, personal

relationships, school, entertainment, dating, work, and so on. Create categories that you think make sense and that you understand.

Option: essay
Use the information you gathered in your journal to write a four- to five-page essay (typed) in which you discuss the ways in which culture affects you. As a rough draft you might consider writing a paragraph for each category you identified above, providing a few examples, and discussing the impact of culture on that area of your life. It might be a good idea to define each cultural element as you begin a discussion of how you are influenced by it.

ACTIVITY 4. 2

Recognizing Ethnocentrism

Most sociologists maintain that each culture is legitimate within its own social context. This view is known as **cultural relativism.** However, sometimes people feel that their culture is the only reality, superior to other cultures, or more correct than others. They may feel that other cultures are strange or they may react negatively to particular elements of another culture. This attitude—known as **ethnocentrism**—is at the heart of many social issues and conflicts, both nationally and globally, professionally and personally. Many times, resolving issues and conflicts in these areas of our lives often requires us to understand and respect a culture different than our own. People from different cultures may have widely divergent ideas, values, and beliefs about things such as gender equality, the family, child rearing, religion, morals, the environment, government, education, health care, and so on. Additionally, they may each have their own symbols, customs, and norms for everyday life.

Journal instructions:
1. For one week keep a journal in which you record ethnocentric comments that you observe: in newspapers, political speeches, classroom discussions and lectures, comments from religious groups and sermons in church, interpersonal interactions, and so on. (Examples: blaming Japanese work ethics for the problems in the U.S. auto industry, criticizing another country's economic or political values, condemning people for having values or sexual orientations different than your own, referring to a religion other than your own as weird, and so on.)

2. Describe the ethnocentric comments that you observe and identify the culture or subculture that is the object of the ethnocentrism.

3. For the ethnocentric comment that you observe, develop an alternative comment that reflects a cultural relativist perspective. (For example, instead

25

of bashing Japanese economic and political values as the reason for their success in the auto industry, you might make a comment about the importance of considering Japanese management styles and how their management styles make sense in terms of their cultural values and beliefs.)

4. Identify three occupations in which using a culturally relativistic point of view is important. Give some examples of how.

Option: class presentation
Prepare a five-minute presentation to your class about what you discussed in your journal.

Option: research paper
Select one of the ethnocentric comments that you observed. Using a culturally relativistic perspective, write a paper (around five pages, typed) in which you analyze the behavior that the comment refers to in terms of the social and cultural context in which it occurs. (For example, you may observe a negative comment about arranged marriages in India. Your task, then, would be to discuss arranged marriages in terms of Indian culture: how they arose, what are their functions, how do they work, and so on). To do this, you will need to conduct some research. Here are some things that you should do:
   a) Look in the library for relevant books or articles about the culture and/or topic in question. Remember that you are likely to obtain less-biased information from a professional journal or a sociology book than from a popular magazine.
   b) Discuss the topic with a professor who may be familiar with the culture or subculture. He or she may also be able to suggest some books or articles that might be helpful.
   c) If possible, discuss the topic with a member of the culture or subculture in question.

ACTIVITY 4. 3

Have A Multicultural Day

Journal instructions:
1. Identify a community in your area that consists of members of a culture or subculture different than yours. Some examples might be an ethnic, racial, or minority neighborhood (Italian, Chinese, Greek, Polish, Hispanic, African or other such communities), a community with a large population of gays and lesbians (for example, Greenwich Village in New York), a religious community (such as the Amish, Mormons, or other religions with nonconventional lifestyles).

2. Spend a total of eight to ten hours observing the community. Keep a detailed written journal of your observations. Here is a list of some things you might do: walk around the neighborhood, eat at a restaurant, note the type of food available and generally purchased, note the types of stores and businesses, browse through the stores, purchase and read a local newspaper, attend a community meeting, have conversations with people you might meet, take note of clothing styles, language, norms, and so on.

3. In your journal, make a list of things (specific behaviors, attitudes, norms, and so on) you observed that you tended to judge negatively or felt were strangely different from your culture. Write a brief paragraph explaining each of your negative judgments. What was it that you reacted to? Why did you feel negative towards it?

4. Examine each of these things in the context of the community's culture. Try to look at each of the things you judged negatively in terms of the cultural context of the community. Write a paragraph in your journal for each in which you try to determine why the behavior, attitude, norm and so on makes sense within the community's cultural context.

Option: essay
Use this information you compiled in your journal (above) to write a four- to five-page essay (typed) in which you describe and analyze the culture or subculture of the community you observed. Be careful not to be judgmental about the community. That is, do not be ethnocentric in your discussion. Rather, analyze the community in terms of its own cultural context and explain how things that might seem strange to outsiders make sense within the specific culture.

ACTIVITY 4. 4

Corporate Cultures

Culture is a concept that is useful in understanding parts of a society as well as whole societies. In recent years, social scientists, administrators, managers, human resource consultants and others have used the concept of culture to understand work organizations. Many companies and corporations have a distinct culture. Their **organizational culture** may determine the organization's management style, productivity, and degree of success. According to research about successful corporations (see for example, Peters and Waterman, 1982; Kanter, 1983), successful organizations tend to have a well-formed, highly-visible culture. The organizations' values, beliefs, norms, symbols, technology and other cultural elements are maintained and transmitted through stories, slogans, myths, and legends (Straus, 1985).

Journal instructions:
1. Record all of the following in your journal. Identify a successful corporation, company, or other organization that you might be interested in working in or simply one that interests you.

2. Ask a career placement counselor at your college for any material (brochures, applications, personnel policies, and so on) available that could provide you with information about the organization.

3. Interview a personnel officer (or human resources officer) and/or an employee at this organization. (This can be done over the telephone if necessary.) Ask them to provide you with any brochures, pamphlets, by-laws, annual reports, or other documents that they can. In addition, ask them the following questions:
   a) Are there any particular values and beliefs that the organization embodies?
   b) How are these values and beliefs present in the everyday operation of the organization?
   c) Does the organization have any heroes or role models that are revered? If so, who are they and why are they revered?
   d) Are there any particular rites of passage, rituals, ceremonies, or norms (for example, hazing, orientation, company parties, and so on) that seem to be distinctly present in the operation of the organization?
   e) Are there any stereotypes of employers, managers, administrators, or other personnel that seem to be held by members of the organization?
   f) Are there any "inside" jokes or "pet peeves" shared by most members of the organization?
   g) Are there any perceived threats from outside that are shared by the organization's members?
   h) Is there a particular language (verbal and/or nonverbal) that members of the organization use to communicate with each other?

4. Summarize what you have found and briefly discuss the culture of the organization in terms of the elements of culture described in your introductory text.

Option: research paper
1. Conduct library research to obtain further information about this organization (or a similar organization) that could help provide you with some insights about its culture. There may be books written about the organization (especially if it is a major corporation such as IBM, Microsoft, General Motors, and so on); articles in newspapers such as The *Wall Street Journal, The New York Times,* or others that deal extensively with businesses; articles in magazines such as *Forbes, Fortune, Businessweek,* or popular news magazines such as *Time* or *Newsweek;* or articles in business journals,

economics journals, or social science journals. Check the appropriate indexes to locate the articles.

2. Using the information that you have obtained so far, write a paper (around five pages, typed) about this organization's culture. Include the following in your essay:
   a) a discussion of the organization's culture (based upon #4 above and in terms of the elements of culture discussed in the chapter on culture in your introductory textbook);
   b) a brief discussion of how your new-found knowledge about this organization's culture might be useful for you in helping you to obtain employment there;
   c) a brief discussion of how understanding this organization's culture, and the concept of organizational culture itself, might help you be more successful in a specific position in which you would like to be hired.

Be sure to provide proper documentation throughout the paper and include a reference (works cited) page.

ACTIVITY 4. 5

Nonverbal Language

How important is nonverbal language in communicating with others? We often realize the importance of nonverbal language when we join a new group or interact with members of a group with which we are not familiar. Just as language is an essential part of a culture's means of symbolic interaction, so is nonverbal language.

Journal instructions:
1. Keep a journal for three days in which you record as many examples as you can of nonverbal communication that you use and that you notice. This can occur anywhere and in any type of situation: at home, at work, at school, in church, at the doctor's office, in the media, in personal relationships, in formal relationships, and so on. The list is likely to be extensive.
   a) What does each of these symbols mean?
   b) How did you learn or come to know what each symbol means?

2. Select five to ten symbols from your list that you use or that you think are used most often and discuss them with two people that are from a culture different than yours. Record their responses in your journal. Ask them:
   a) if they know what each of the symbols means.
   b) if in their culture they have a way of nonverbally communicating a similar idea and, if so, what is it?

c) to give you some examples of nonverbal expressions commonly used within their culture.

Option: class presentation
Make a brief presentation of your findings to your class. You might begin your presentation with a "quiz" to see how many people can identify and understand the examples of nonverbal language that you obtained from your interviews.

ACTIVITY 4. 6

Bilingualism

Bilingualism can be loosely defined as the use of two or more languages. Issues concerning bilingualism have long been debated in the United States. Should English should be the official language of the United States, or should one or more other languages be accepted and widely used? Should there be bilingual voting ballots? Should immigrants be required to pass an English-language proficiency exam? One of the most hotly-debated bilingualism issues is whether or not education should be bilingual.

Journal instructions:
1. Spend three to four hours observing in an elementary school with bilingual programs and three to four hours observing in an elementary school without bilingual programs. You may need to call your local Board of Education to find out what the nearest schools are that offer bilingual education. Obtain the permission of the school principals before you begin your observations. Try to obtain information about the following (record your observations in your journal):
   a) classroom structure (for example, seating arrangements, decorations, material on bulletin boards or walls, and so on);
   b) racial and ethnic composition of the student body;
   c) racial and ethnic composition of the faculty;
   d) the curriculum;
   e) books;
   f) non-academic activities (lunch, recreation time, clubs, and so on);
   g) interaction among peers;
   h) amount of class participation by English and limited English-proficiency students.

2. Interview an administrator (for example, principal or assistant principal), a guidance counselor, and/or a teacher from each school. Ask them the following questions and record their answers in your journal:
   a) how successful they feel the overall academic program at the school is;

30

b) if they feel the needs of all students are being met:
c) how they feel about bilingual education;
d) what the views of the members of the community are about bilingual education;
e) how the faculty feels about bilingual education;
f) whether or not they think that their school should continue, or should establish, bilingual programs;
g) what they feel the pros and cons of bilingual education are.

3. Read the section in your introductory text that discusses the **Sapir-Whorf Hypothesis,** the idea that language influences the way people perceive the world around them. Use this idea to explain why bilingual education is such an important sociological issue.

4. Based upon your observations and interviews, briefly discuss, in your journal, what you think the advantages and disadvantages of bilingual education are and why this is such an important sociological issue.

Option: research paper
1. Conduct library research to find arguments for and against bilingual education. Use the appropriate indexes and reference material to help you find four to six articles about bilingual education. Excellent discussions are found in Eshleman, Cashion, and Basirico (1993); Romaine (1989); Stoller (1976); Hakuta (1986); Henry (1990); Haugen (1987); Bernstein (1990); and many others.

2. Based upon your observations and interviews (from your journal) and your library research, write an essay (about five to seven pages, typed) in which you compare similarities, differences, advantages, and disadvantages of bilingual and monolingual programs.

CHAPTER 5

Social Structure, Social Groups and Social Organizations

Society is more than the sum of separate individuals behaving, thinking, and feeling freely and randomly. Rather, society consists of patterns of relationships that influence and, often, determine the way we think, act, and feel. Sociologists refer to the totality of these patterns of relationships as a **social structure.** The basic components of social structure that sociologists study are statuses, roles, norms, groups, organizations, and institutions. For sociologists, one of the most important ways of understanding and explaining human behavior, thought, and emotion is through understanding and explaining the social structure of the society in which they live.

ACTIVITY 5.1

The Influence Of Social Structure On Your Everyday Life

Popular explanations of human behavior are usually in psychological terms such as personality, motivation, attitudes, unconscious drives, and so on. By contrast, the sociological view is that individual and social behavior are shaped largely through social structure. Sociologists do not deny the validity and usefulness of many psychological theories and concepts, In fact, there are quite a few areas in which these two disciplines overlap and share each other's ideas. However, sociologists look first and foremost at humans as social beings.

Journal instructions:
For one complete day, keep a journal in which you reflect on how different aspects of social structure influence how you think, act, and feel in various situations and at various times throughout the day. Consider the impact of the following aspects of social structure on the way you think, act, and feel:

32

statuses, roles, norms, primary groups, secondary groups, in-groups, out-groups, reference groups, relative deprivation, role conflict, role strain, role ambiguity, and any other aspects of social structure that you find relevant. (Read about these concepts in your introductory sociology textbook.)

For example, you got up at seven a.m. today because your student status requires you to be in class at eight a.m. Your decision of what to wear today was influenced by your status as sorority or fraternity pledge (also a reference group). Yet, you couldn't help but think about how members of another primary group in which you are a member, your church group back home, might judge this style of dress. You faced a role conflict. Since your church group had no power over you at the moment, you opted to conform to the Greek dress code. Your examples may be much more complex or simple than this example. You will see, though, that nearly all of your thoughts, feelings, and actions are influenced by elements of the social structure.

Do not treat anything as insignificant. The possible topics to discuss are innumerable. Do not wait until the end of the day to write about your observations. Take notes and make comments in your journal continuously as you go through your day. Remember, you only have to continue this activity for one day, so please bear with the inconvenience and be thorough in your observations of how social structure influences you.

Option: essay
Use your journal to write an essay (around five pages, typed) in which you present a sociological analysis of a day in your life. If you have done your journal correctly, you will likely have too many experiences to include in a five-page paper. Select the ones that will best help you with your analysis of how your life is influenced by the social structure.

ACTIVITY 5. 2

Role Ambiguity, Role Strain, and Role Conflict

Much of the psychological distress that we must deal with is the result of the statuses we occupy and their associated roles. They may lead to role ambiguity, role conflict, or role strain.

Role ambiguity occurs when the expectations of a role are not clear. Thus, we may not understand what is expected of us. For example, "I want to have a non-traditional relationship with my spouse, but I am not always sure how I am supposed to act."

33

Role strain results from having a role overload or from having roles with contradictory expectations. There is simply not enough time and energy to meet the expectations of two or more roles. For example, "I have to study for an exam tonight (student role), but my boss wants me to work late (employee role)."

Role conflict is when the demands of two or more roles are incompatible. It usually occurs when the values of one role are in conflict with the values of another. For example, "As an artist I am supposed to be creative and innovative (artist role), but as a parent I may have to subject myself to commercialism in order to help support my family (parent role)."

Journal instructions:
1. For one week keep a journal in which you record the problems, crises, and stress that you face that result from role ambiguity, role strain, and/or role conflict. Explain how each problem is related to role expectations.

2. Looking at each problem as a result of status or role, suggest some ways to solve them.

Option: class presentation
Prepare a five-minute presentation in which you discuss how the problems you faced during your week of observation were related to status and role.

Option: bibliography
After you do your journal, conduct library research to develop a bibliography of around ten articles from sociology journals that deal with issues related to status or role ambiguity, conflict, or strain. Use the bibliographic format contained in the journal articles as a model for the way in which your bibliography should be arranged (and/or see Activity 1. 3).

Option: research paper
Complete the above bibliography. Then select a few (two or more) articles from your bibliography that can provide you with insights about one of the problems you discussed in your journal. Write a paper (around four to five pages, typed) in which you use material from the journal articles you selected to discuss the problem you selected from your journal

ACTIVITY 5. 3

How Social Life Is Organized

The term **social organization** is used in sociology in two different ways. One way refers to a specific entity such as a formal organization (for example, a school, hospital, country club, prison, and so on). The other refers to the way a society, institution, group, or formal organization is arranged (organized).

Journal instructions:
1. For one week, be a participant observer of a group in which you are a member in order to analyze how it is organized and how its organization affects the members in the group. Select a group that interacts frequently (preferably, at least once a day) such as a family, fraternity or sorority, sports team, work group, club, or other such groups. (If you do not understand participation observation method of research, reread the section in the methods chapter of your introductory sociology text. You may also want to consult a sociology or social science research methods text.)

2. At various times during your involvement with the group, or immediately after, take notes about your observations of how the group is organized, how the members are affected by the organization, and the insights about the group you develop as a result of your participant observation. Focus on the following: type of group (and how this affects the way the group is organized and the members), statuses, roles, norms, role conflicts, role strain, role ambiguity, and any other concepts you think are relevant to understanding the group's organization. If you are unsure of what these concepts mean, read about them in your introductory sociology book.

3. Draw a sociogram to describe the types of relationships between the members of the group. A **sociogram** is a diagram that usually uses circles (one for each group member) and arrows (indicating the flow of interaction between two or more members) to describe the patterns of interaction among members of a group. Look in an introductory sociology text or ask your professor to provide you with an example, or see the discussion by Moreno (1934) who introduced the concept of sociograms.

Option: research paper
1. Conduct library research to locate two or more sociological articles or books about the type of group you have been observing. Use these sources to help provide additional insights or to help you explain the group's social organization or some aspect of it that you observed.

2. Integrating your journal material and your library research, write an essay (around four to five pages, typed) in which you discuss the social organization of the group you studied. Besides describing the way the group is organized, use one or more of the major theoretical perspectives in sociology (discussed in your introductory sociology textbook's chapter on theory) to help you explain the processes taking place within the group. Be sure to cite your sources properly throughout the essay and include a reference (works cited) page.

ACTIVITY 5. 4

Using Knowledge Of Social Structure To Assess Problems In The Workplace

An important way to use knowledge about social structure is in assessing problems in the workplace (such as low productivity, failure to achieve the organization's goals, low employee morale, conflict between employees, and so forth). It may be useful to look at the work setting as an arrangement of formally- and informally-defined statuses and role expectations rather than as separate individuals working in the same place. A long-standing debate between sociologists and psychologists is whether the individual shapes the role or the role shapes the individual. Although the debate may never be resolved, sociologists (and some psychologists) have found that in many instances, role expectations play the more important part in shaping individual and social behavior. This has been found to be true especially in work settings.

A classic example of using knowledge of organizational structure to examine problems in a work setting is William Whyte's (1949) study of the restaurant industry. Whyte was hired as a consultant for a restaurant chain that was having problems with inefficiency, low worker morale, and high employee turnover. He found that role ambiguity among waiters, waitresses, and kitchen workers - not personality conflicts - accounted for the personal anxiety and interpersonal conflicts among the staff in many restaurants. His solution - as obvious as it may seem now, it had a major impact on the restaurant industry in 1949 - was to create clear, specific roles for each of the different types of employees in the restaurants.

Journal instructions:

1. Select an occupational setting in which your or someone you know works (for example, a friend, parent, or other relative) for the purpose of examining its organizational structure.

2. Find an occupational setting in which you will be able to: observe the work setting for three to four hours, interview two or three employees, and read available reports, bulletin boards, policy statements, organization charts, and other documents that might be available to the public or to personnel. Use **each** of these methods in order to find out (and record in your journal) the following:
   a) What are the organization's objectives and/or goals?
   b) What is the social structure of the work setting like? (What are the formal and/or informal statuses and role expectations? How are they arranged? How are the work tasks organized? Is there a specific, clearly-defined routine?)

c) Identify the types of personnel conflicts that occur and what the source of them may be. (Do they result from role ambiguity, role conflict, or role strain? Are they the result of competition between various primary groups within the setting? Are there in-group/out-group tensions that exist? And so on).

d) Are personnel conflicts addressed by the administrators or others? If so, how?

Option: essay

Write a four- to five-page essay (typed), in which you discuss the organizational structure of the work setting you studied. Discuss it in terms of the journal criteria (above) and other relevant aspects from the chapter on social structure in your introductory text. In addition, explain why you feel the situation needs no improvement, works well but could be improved, or has serious problems in terms of structure (roles, status, organizational structure, etc.). Why? What could be done to alter the structure to improve the way it works?

ACTIVITY 5. 5

Comparing Organizations With Different Degrees Of Bureaucracy

One characteristic of modern complex societies is the presence of bureaucracies. A bureaucracy is a formal, relatively rigid organizational structure that involves clearly-defined patterns of activity in order to accomplish the organization's goals. Bureaucracies typically have the following clearly stipulated characteristics: a division of labor, a hierarchy of authority, public (rather than private) record of all files and transactions, employment based on merit selection, a set of objective rules and regulations for the organization's activities, and career expectations of employees. Review the section on bureaucracy in your introductory textbook for an explanation of these items.

The effectiveness of the bureaucratic organizational structure sometimes comes at the cost of de-personalization of employees or of the people with which the organization serves. All of us have experienced the frustrations of finding our way through the maze of bureaucratic "red tape" at one time or another: at the Department of Motor Vehicles (or any government office), at registration for courses, in the emergency room at the hospital, and so on. Despite the drawbacks of the bureaucratic structure in some situations (see the discussion in your text about dysfunctions of bureaucracies), sociologists generally consider the bureaucratic style to be the most effective way for many complex organizations to operate.

Journal instructions:
1. Identify a highly bureaucratic organization and a less formal organization that performs similar functions in your area (for example, a grocery chain and a small family-operated grocery store, a large hospital or medical practice and a private doctor's office, H&R Block and a private accountant's office, a large law firm and a one-attorney law office, and so forth.)

2. Interview someone employed in each business. Ask them the following questions and record their answers in your journal. After each question ask them what they feel are any advantages or disadvantages of the approach to running the organization in this way.
   a) What are the overall objectives of the organization?
   b) Are employees hired to perform specific tasks, or are they assigned tasks as need arises?
   c) Is there a clear and stated hierarchy of authority in this organization?
   d) Does the business belong to (is it owned by) an organization, or to individuals?
   e) Are the business' records, files, and accounts kept in a separate location from the employees' homes?
   f) How much influence does the organization have over the employees' private lives?
   g) Is there a consistent, formal set of rules and regulations for specific situations or tasks?
   h) Are people hired, fired, and promoted based upon merit or upon some form of favoritism?
   i) Are there records kept of all transactions that take place?
   j) Is there an expectation of employees that they have a long term commitment to the organization?

3. Observe the daily routine of the organization, or one part of the organization, for one to two hours on two separate occasions (total of two to four hours). Record your observations in your journal. Use your opportunity to observe to obtain any additional answers or insights to the items in question two above.

Option: essay
Write a four- to five-page essay, typed, in which you compare the way each of the organizations you studied meets its objectives. In your essay, compare the merits of using a bureaucratic or non-bureaucratic structure in meeting the organizations' goals. Are there any situations in which either of the organizations might benefit from using a more bureaucratic or less bureaucratic approach? Relate your discussion to ideas from the section in bureaucracy in your introductory text.

ACTIVITY 5. 6

How Does The Bureaucratization Of Society Affect Personal Life

Richard Hall (1987) says, "Organizations surround us; we are born in them and usually die in them; the space in between is filled with them. They are just about impossible to escape. They are inevitable" (p. 1). In addition to the development of an "organizational society," organizations are becoming increasingly bureaucratized in order to meet the complex demands of society. As Charles Perrow (1986) notes, "We have constructed a society where the satisfaction of our wants as consumers largely depends on restricting the employees who do the producing" (p. 5). For example, many organizations today have mandatory drug testing for their employees. Thus, since we live in a society in which organizations surround us, society itself is becoming increasingly bureaucratized.

Journal instructions:
Identify five people that are employed by highly bureaucratic organizations (large companies such as IBM, General Motors, large universities, and so on.) Ask each of them the following questions and record their answers in your journal:

a) Are there any policies where you work that affect your personal and private life?

b) Can you tell me what they are?

c) Do you feel that these policies are necessary in order to help the organization meet its goals or do you feel that they unnecessarily intrude on people's lives?

d) Do you feel that if you have something valuable to say about the way the organization is run that someone would be receptive to hearing it?

e) Do you feel that the organization has more control over your life than you would like?

Option: essay
Use the material in your introductory text about the advantages, disadvantages, functions and dysfunctions of bureaucracy and your journal interviews to write an essay (around three to five pages, typed) in which you discuss your impressions about how our lives are affected b y bureaucratization.

CHAPTER 6

Socialization and Social Interaction

A long-standing controversy in studies of human behavior is the nature vs. nurture debate. Do humans develop their individual and social traits as a result of a genetic predisposition or is it a result of interaction with other humans? Most sociologists do not deny that biological makeup provides the potential for the way in which humans develop. However, sociologists contend that human interaction is responsible for the way in which that biological potential is shaped. Without human interaction, any potential provided by an individual's biological makeup (including the ability to think) would not develop.

Socialization is the term that sociologists use to refer to the process of human development. More generally, socialization refers to the processes whereby individuals are encouraged, intentionally or unintentionally, to learn about and conform to the culture (norms, symbols, values, beliefs, and so on) of the society or group in which they are becoming a member. Besides learning the ways of the group or society through socialization, socialization contributes to the individual's sense of **self.**

The **self** is perhaps the central sociological concept in the study of socialization and social interaction. The sociological concept of self refers to the combination of perspectives that we hold toward our own being, others, and the world. It is the way we think about who we are and, as a result, how we approach the world. The self is considered to be a **social self** because it arises and is shaped through socialization and social interaction.

ACTIVITY 6. 1

Socialization And The Self Throughout Life

Socialization is a process that continues throughout our lives. It continues as long as we face new conditions to which we must adapt, enter a new status, learn new roles, and interact with others. As a result, our sense of self changes throughout our lives.

Journal instructions:
1. In your journal, identify what you think are the most important characteristics of your self and your personality. (For example, are you shy, creative, spiritual, ambitious, insecure, and so on? Are you interested in music, politics, sports, art, and so on? Are you liberal, conservative, middle of the road?) In other words, describe what you are like and the image you have of your self.

2. Go to your introductory text book's chapter on socialization and read about the various theories and agents of socialization. In your journal, discuss the following:
   a) How did the various agents of socialization lead you to develop your characteristics and image of your self? Provide specific examples.
   b) Use Cooley's "looking glass self" theory, Mead's "role taking" theory, and other relevant theories of socialization that your chapter discusses to analyze the characteristics and image of your self.

Option: essay
Write an essay (around four to five pages, typed) in which you use the theories and ideas contained within the chapter on socialization in your text to examine how you developed these characteristics of your self you mentioned in your journal.

ACTIVITY 6. 2

Social Interaction And The Self

According to Erving Goffman, social interaction is essentially a performance. We try to present ourselves in a particular way by preparing beforehand and by employing tactics during an interaction to manage the impression we are trying to convey to others and to maintain a particular definition of a situation. From this point of view, social interaction becomes a form of self socialization as we work to convince ourselves and others that we are a certain type of person.

Journal instructions:
1. Read the introduction (pp. 1 to 15) to Erving Goffman's book *The Presentation of Self in Everyday Life* (1959) and the sections about Goffman in your introductory textbook. (The introduction to Goffman's *Presentation of Self* also appears in many introduction to sociology readers such as Henslin, 1991; Clark and Robboy, 1988; and others.)

2. In your journal, summarize and discuss, in your own words, Goffman's central thesis and concepts discussed in the introduction to his book and in your text.

3. Keep a journal for one full day in which you analyze all of your interactions in terms of Goffman's ideas. That is, keep track of how your behavior is like a performance.

Option: essay
Using the novelistic incident about Preedy that Goffman cites on p. 5 of his book as a model, write a brief essay (around two to three pages, typed) in which you describe one of the incidents that you recorded in your journal.

Option: class presentation
Make brief presentation to your class about Goffman's ideas and illustrate them with one or two of the incidents you analyzed in your journal.

Option: research paper
1. Read Erving Goffman's book *The Presentation of Self in Everyday Life* (1959) in its entirety.

2. Summarize Goffman's central thesis and identify the ways in which social interaction is a like a performance (that is, summarize the central ideas in each chapter).

3. Write a five- to seven-page paper (typed) in which you use Goffman's ideas to analyze and discuss in depth an interaction setting in which you were involved (family dinner, party, meeting your boyfriend's or girlfriend's parents, a religious ceremony, and so on. Be creative and have fun with this.) In your paper, include specific quotes and references to Goffman's book.

ACTIVITY 6. 3

Socialization And Child Care Programs

Child care has become a major issue in American society. Part of the issue is political: Should there be a national child care policy which provides sufficient resources to ensure affordable, available, high quality non-parental child care programs? Opponents to such a policy argue that child care remains the primary responsibility of the parents and therefore government should not play a significant role in supporting child care programs. Supporters of a national day care policy argue that the government must take steps to ensure adequate child care programs.

Underlying the political questions, though, are sociological ones. What is the impact on the child of being socialized in non-parental child care settings? Is it different than being socialized in the home? If so, are the differences beneficial or detrimental to the development of the child? Many social scientists feel that to answer questions such as these we must examine the structural factors of child care settings that shape the socialization process and its impact on children. According to Browne-Miller (1990), these include such things as: the ratio of caregivers to children (that is, the number of children per caregiver), the personalities of the caregivers, the demographics of the caregiving population (for example, age, gender, race), the overall philosophy of the child-care team, the use of unstructured versus structured time, the attention given to discipline and rules, the personal and emotional involvement of the caregivers, the attention given to preventive and recuperative health care, the overall environment in which the care takes place, and many other factors.

Journal instructions:
1. Identify a child care center nearby in which you will be able to observe and interview people.

2. In your journal, make a list of the structural factors you wish to examine. Include the above items suggested by Browne-Miller and any additional ones you think might have an impact on the way in which children are socialized. You may get some additional ideas from reading the chapter on socialization in your introductory text.

3. Ask the director of the child care center you identified for permission to observe at the center for a sociology assignment. Assure the director that the information you collect is solely for the purposes of this assignment and will be held in strict confidence.

4. Conduct observations of the child care center for at least five hours. Record your observations in your journal. You may want to break your observations up into two separate visits. After your first visit, think about whether or not you are obtaining the data you want. If not, figure out what you need to do to obtain the data. Reflect on what you have observed so far. Develop some tentative insights and conclusions. This will make your second visit much more productive.

5. In addition to your observation, interview the director (or available administrator) and a caregiver who works there after you have made your observations. Use these interviews to find out the answers to any questions that you were unable to obtain from your observations or to verify some of your observations.

Option: essay
Carefully re-read the chapter on socialization in your introductory textbook. Write an essay (around three to five pages, typed) in which you use the theories and ideas in the chapter as the basis for a discussion of the socialization setting (i.e., the child care center) you observed. That is, apply the theories and ideas in the chapter to think about and discuss how the structural factors affect the way the children are socialized.

Option: research paper
1. Conduct library research to identify and discuss the major dimensions or developmental concerns of non-parental child care that social scientists have studied. There are many good books and professional journal articles that address the topic of non-parental child care. (See, for example, Eshleman et al., 1993; Belsky, 1990; Browne-Miller, 1990; Clarke-Stewart, 1989; Kagan and Newton, 1989; Kontos, 1990; Leavitt and Power, 1989; Phillips et al, 1987; Ruopp et al., 1979; Siegel, 1990; Whitebook et al, 1989; and many others). Use your library to obtain four or five books and/or articles on this topic. Identify and discuss the major concerns that social scientists have about socialization of children in non-parental settings.

2. Write a five- to seven-page paper, typed, in which you use the theories and ideas in the chapter on socialization in your introductory text, relevant ideas from your library research, and information that you obtained in your journal to discuss what you think are some possible socialization outcomes of the child care center you studied. Be sure to document your references correctly and include a works cited page.

ACTIVITY 6. 4

Gender Role Socialization in Everyday Life

Gender roles are expectations associated with being male and female. As with all roles, these are learned through the socialization process. Gender role socialization, then, refers to all the ways in which we are socialized into being male or female. The result is that we internalize norms, values, beliefs, and perspectives of our respective gender and, indeed, become male or female. The sociological explanation of why males act, think, and see like males and why females act, think, and see like females is because we are socialized into these roles from birth to death.

Journal instructions:
1. You can do this journal activity anywhere: at home, at work, in school on vacation, and so on. Before you begin, read the sections about socialization and gender role socialization in your introductory text (in the chapter on

socialization and also in the chapter on gender) about the ways in which gender role socialization takes place. Make a list of these in your journal.

2. For one week, keep a journal in which you record as thoroughly as possible every instance of gender role socialization that you experience and that you observe in your everyday activities. These include observations of interpersonal relationships (yours and others around you), family, friends, advertisements, school, media (television, radio, newspapers, magazines), and so on. Briefly describe each situation and event and discuss the underlying gender role message being sent.

3. At the end of the week, do a content analysis of your journal. That is, organize the types of socialization experiences that you recorded into categories (for example, everyday interaction, media, religion, family, etc.).

Option: essay
Write a four- to five-page essay, typed, in which you use the theories of socialization to discuss the observations you made in your journal throughout the week.

ACTIVITY 6. 5

Gender Role Socialization And The Mass Media

The mass media - including television, radio, popular books and magazines, newspapers, and movies - is one of the most powerful agents of gender role socialization. American adults spend approximately two and one half hours a day - over one half of their leisure time - watching television. Children age two through five spend an average of twenty-seven hours a week in front of the television (Moody, 1980). Think of the impact that television alone, not to mention other media, has on our selves.

If possible (and if your professor requires you to), read Erving Goffman's book *Gender Advertisements* (1979) before beginning this activity.

Journal instructions:
1. For one week, watch commercial television (that is, not a public broadcasting network, such as PBS) for at least one to two hours a day. Vary the times that you watch it. Sometimes watch during evening prime time, sometimes during the day, and so on.

2. In your journal, keep an organized and detailed record of all of the programs and all of the commercials that you observe during the period in which you are watching television. Note:

45

a) the time of day
b) the program or commercial
c) the theme of the program or the type of product in the commercial
d) the roles of the males and females
e) the characteristics that they are displaying (sexy, macho, nurturing, emotional, instrumental, and so on)
e) the relationship between the males and the females (are they portrayed as equals? If not, who is dominant?)
f) who the program or commercial is designed to appeal to
g) examples of comments or behaviors that tend to portray males and/or females as being a certain way
h) any other aspects of the program or commercial that you think are a form of gender role socialization

Option: essay
Use your journal observations to write an essay (around three to five pages, typed) in which you discuss the way in which television is an agent of gender role socialization.

ACTIVITY 6. 6

Gender Role Socialization In The Classroom

Education is another area in which social scientists have found much gender role socialization taking place (for example, Serbin and O'Leary, 1975; Sadker and Sadker, 1985, 1986). Myra and David Sadker, two educational psychologists, studied the differential treatment of males and females in the classroom. Among other things, they looked at the type of attention and interaction that males and females receive from the teachers. In one study, they looked at how often males and females were called upon in class and how they were responded to by the teachers. They categorized the types to responses the teachers made as follows:
a) *praise* - teacher commends the student on the answer (for example, "Excellent work John", "You are right on target, Mary"; and so on)
b) *acceptance* - teacher simply acknowledges the answer, whether it is correct or incorrect (for example, teacher nods or makes non-committal comments like, "Uh-huh"; "Hmmm"; and so on)
c) *remediation* - teacher provides guidance to the student (for example, "Okay. You're on the right track. But take it one step further"; "Not quite. But try looking at it this way"; and so on)
d) *criticism* - teacher berates the student for giving an incorrect answer (for example, "It's time to start taking your assignments seriously"; "Maybe if you would come to class on time you might understand what we are doing"; and so on)

Observation and journal instructions:

1. Identify four different classes at your college or another college, a high school, or a middle school in your area that you will be able to observe. Do not select classes in which you are a student. They must be different subjects, have a mixture of male and female students, and must be discussion-type classes of around forty students or less (that is, not large lecture hall classes).

2. Prepare coding sheets that you will use to help you record what you see. Here is how:

   a) At the top of a sheet of paper, list the following: name of the course; gender of instructor; number of males in class; and number of females in class.

   b) Then, create columns going across the page from left to right, with the following headings: male; female; praises; accepts; remediates; criticizes; and miscellaneous.

3. Make about twenty copies of these sheets. You should have about five sheets available for each class you observe.

4. Use these sheets to record the ways that teachers act toward students during each class period. Each time a professor calls on a student, indicate whether he or she calls on a male or a female by placing a check in the appropriate column. After the student is called upon, indicate the professor's response by placing a a check in **one or more** of the columns indicating "praise," "accept", "remediate", or "criticize." (See the introduction to this activity for examples of each.) In the "miscellaneous" column, you can write down any additional information that you think might be meaningful; for example, the topic of the question, the difficulty of the question, and so on. This is going to occur very quickly. In a single class period, do not be surprised if you have dozens of responses or more to code. So, be prepared and be alert.

Here is an example of what one of your coding sheets might look like after a few questions are asked:

Course:_____ English literature
Gender of instructor: male
Number of males:_____ 18
Number of females:___ 17

male	female	praises	accepts	remediates	criticizes	misc.
X		X				
	X		X			
	X				X	
X		X		X		
etc.						

47

5. In your journal, summarize the data (that is, the results of your observations) from your coding sheets. For example, count how many times a professor called upon a male and how many times the professor called upon a female. Count how many times males received praise and how many times females received praise, and so on. There are many ways to summarize the data. These are only a few.

6. Once you summarize the data, try to interpret them. What do the data you collected tell you about the way males and females are treated in different types of courses? Are they treated the same? If not, what are the differences?

7. Examine the textbooks used in each of the courses you observed to see if there is any gender bias. You do not have to read the entire books. Pick out a sample chapter.
    a) Do they use generic pronouns to refer to both genders ("it"; "they"; "them"; and so on), have a balance between using masculine and feminine pronouns ("he"; "she"; "him"; "her"), or is there a tendency to use predominantly masculine pronouns when both genders are meant?
    b) Do the examples in the book that refer to humans tend to place people into stereotypical traditional gender roles (such as referring to male doctors, female elementary school teachers, mothers who are parents, fathers who "work", and so on)?

Option: essay
Use your observational data and your analysis of the course textbooks that you did to write a paper (around five pages, typed) in which you discuss gender role socialization in the classroom. Incorporate theories of socialization from your textbook (such as Cooley's "looking glass self", Mead's "role taking," and other relevant theories) into your discussion.

CHAPTER 7

Deviance and Social Control

Sociologists generally define **deviance** as variation from a set of shared norms or shared social expectations. Hence, from the sociological perspective, no acts or people are deviant in and of themselves.

The sociological perspective on deviant behavior is different than traditional perspectives on deviance. Traditional perspectives on deviance tend to look at people or behaviors as deviant. One traditional perspective, the **absolutist and moral view,** assumes that particular acts or people are deviant in all contexts and these acts and people are bad and immoral. A second traditional perspective on deviance, the **medical model,** suggests that deviants are sick people, deviance is unhealthy, and a preponderance of deviance is evidence of a sick society. A third perspective, the **statistical model,** defines deviance as any behavior that is statistically atypical, that is, behavior that varies from the average or mode.

By contrast, the sociological perspective is a **relativistic view.** From this perspective, deviance does not refer to a particular type of act nor does it refer to particular types of people, without considering the social and cultural context. Rather, deviance is seen as a relative condition that varies according to time, place, situation in which the behavior occurs, and the status of the person engaged in the behavior. The sociological perspective takes into account the great diversity of meanings that can be associated with people or acts in different situations. In other words, acts or people that are considered deviant in one context might not be considered deviant in another. No people or actions are inherently deviant.

This perspective on deviance opens up a variety of interesting and important questions. How does the meaning of particular types of behavior or the people who engage in them become defined as deviant? Who has the power to control what is and what is not defined as deviant in a society? How and why do people come to violate the norms in a particular social and cultural

49

context?   Why are some forms of deviance punished and others not? What are the consequences   (positive and negative) of deviance for a society? These are only a few of the questions about deviance that the sociological perspective raises.   Answering questions such as these is important not only for gaining a better understanding of human behavior, but for establishing social policies that are intended to benefit society.

ACTIVITY 7. 1

Comparing Traditional And Relativist Views On Deviance

As mentioned above, the traditional views on deviance tend to focus primarily on the act and/or the actor(s). Sociological views do not neglect the act and/or the actor, but place the major emphasis on what the behavior means in a particular context. When and where did the behavior take place? What was the nature or context of the situation in which it took place? What was the status of the person (or people) engaged in the behavior? Who is the audience that views the behavior? It is necessary to answer these questions before the meaning of the behavior can be determined.

Journal instructions:
1. Identify one behavior or lifestyle that is often depicted in the news as immoral, sick, or deviant (for example, homosexuality, various forms of sexual behavior, drug use, countercultural groups such as "Dead Heads", homeless people, and so on). Pick a group that interests you.

2. Look through current and back issues of national and/or local daily newspapers to find at least five news items (news articles, editorials, essays, letters to the editor, and so on) about the behavior or lifestyle you identified.

3. In your journal, discuss the content of **each** of the news items (using quotes and excerpts when appropriate) in terms of the following:
   a) Briefly summarize what the article (news report, essay, letter to the editor, and so on) is about.
   b) What is the author's source of information?
   c)   Did the author use any specific research methods to obtain the information? If so, explain.
   d) Is the "deviance" explained predominantly in terms of types of people, types of behavior, or social context in which it occurs?
   e) Is there any attempt to examine the social meaning of the deviance (that is, what the behavior or lifestyle means within a specific social or cultural context, to the people engaged in the behavior, to a society, or to a culture)?
   f) Is the behavior or lifestyle in question depicted from a traditional view (absolutist, moralist, medical, or statistical views) or a relativist view?

g) Summarize the author's conclusions.

h) What is the overall impression given by the author about the behavior or lifestyle in question (for example, sick, immoral, evil, creative, innovative, appropriate, necessary, and so on)? In other words, what is the impression that the reader is left with about the deviance after reading the news item?

Option: research essay

1. Locate two or three articles in <u>sociology</u> journals that discuss the behavior or lifestyle you selected. Use the *Social Science Index* or *Sociological Abstracts* (or other relevant indexes in your library) to help you locate these articles. Answer the questions provided in the above journal instructions about each article and include these answers in your journal.

2. Imagine that you are a journalist writing an article or an essay for a newspaper or a popular magazine. Write an essay or news story (about four to five pages, typed) in which you integrate sociological theories and viewpoints into your report about the event you are covering.

ACTIVITY 7. 2

**Using Sociological Research And Knowledge
To Understand A Deviant Group**

Your introductory textbook discusses a number of theories of deviance that can be used to understand "alternative lifestyles":

Anomie theory examines behavior in terms of conflicts that occur between culturally-valued goals and institutionalized means of achieving them.

Conflict theories say that definitions of deviance are devised by the powerful to repress and exploit the powerless or the underclass.

Sociocultural learning theories, such as **cultural transmission theory, differential association theory,** and **learning theory** focus on the social and psychological processes in which deviant behavior is learned and transmitted.

Labeling theory focuses on how behavior comes to be defined as deviant and what the effects of being labeled deviant are.

Go to the chapter on deviance in your introductory sociology text and carefully study these theories.

Journal instructions:

1. Find someone you know (an informant) that engages in behavior, activity, or lifestyle that is generally considered to be deviant by the predominant norms of the society and culture in which you live. Examples: illegal drug users, nudists, homosexuals, prostitutes, members of religious cults, Hell's Angels, Ku Klux Klan members, and so on.

2. In your journal, make a list of questions about the group that you might ask from the point of view of **each** of the theories. (For example, using anomie theory you might want to ask: What are the goals and values of the members of the group? Do they accept or reject the dominant culture's values and goals regarding a particular behavior, say, sexuality? And so on. Using labeling theory you might ask: How is the group defined or labeled by other groups in society? By what criteria is the group labeled as deviant? Who has labeled the group as deviant? What is the effect of being labeled deviant on group members? And so on.) There are many questions that you can develop using each theory as the basis. Take great care with this part of the activity because it will determine the types of things you will look for in your research.

3. Ask your informant to take you to a meeting, convention, rally, or some other situation open to the public in which you can observe the group (for example: Grateful Dead concert, homosexual pride parade or gay bar, nudist beach, and so on). Your purpose in observing the group is to try to obtain answers to the questions that you developed above by observing the group, talking to its members, reading literature that they may have about them, and so on. Not all of the questions will apply, nor will you be able to answer all of them. Use them as a general guide for your observations. Obtain as much information about the group's norms, values, and beliefs as possible. Try to see the situation from the point of view of someone who is a member of the group. Your goal is to try to determine what it is like to the members of the group to be in that group. Observe the group on more than one occasion if possible. Be sure to keep detailed notes in your journal about what you observe and find out.

4. In your journal, briefly discuss (based upon your observations) which sociological theories of deviance you think are the most relevant for understanding the group you are studying.

Option: research paper

1. Conduct library research in which you obtain three to four articles or books written by sociologists about the type of group you observed. Use these resources to help you answer your questions about the group.

2. Write a five- to seven-page paper (typed) in which you discuss the group by using relevant sociological theories, the information that you collected in your journal, and information you obtained from your library research. Be sure to document all of your sources correctly and include a reference (works cited) page.

ACTIVITY 7. 3

Applying Theories Of Deviance To Crime And Delinquency

As with other types of deviance that are reported in the news, acts of crime and delinquency are often described in terms of the act or the actor. Consideration of sociological theories is rarely given in the news. Sociological theories of deviance can often provide important insights about criminal and delinquent acts.

Journal instructions:

1. For one week, record in your journal all articles about crime and delinquent behavior that appear in a local and national daily newspaper.

2. For **each** crime or delinquent act, identify one or more theories of deviance that could be used to examine it and explain how. For example, an executive of a company is caught embezzling funds. Which theories of deviance could be used to examine this crime? In terms of Merton's anomie theory of deviance, the crime might be examined by looking at which mode of adaptation (conformist, innovator, ritualist, retreatist, or rebel) the criminal may have. What other theories of deviance could be used to examine the criminal behavior? Discuss these in your journal.

Option: essay
1. Arrange all of the incidents of crime and delinquency that you recorded in your journal into types—for example, murder, theft, assault, and so on.

2. Using your journal for supporting material, write an essay (around five pages, typed) in which you discuss which theories of deviance are the most useful for understanding each of the different types of crime and delinquency you categorized.

Option: research paper
Locate four or five articles from <u>sociology</u> journals about one of the types of crime you identified above. Write a paper (around five to seven pages, typed) in which you use the sociology articles to explain the current examples of this crime that you found in newspaper. Some issues to address are: What are the

differences between the news accounts and the sociological explanations of the crime? What variables are used in the sociology articles to help explain the crime? What sociological theories were used in the articles that could help you explain the crime you selected? What statistics or other facts are relevant to explaining the crime? And so on. Do not necessarily limit yourself to these questions.

ACTIVITY 7. 4

Curtailing Drug Abuse: Internal Control Or External Control

Although deviance is universal and does serve some positive social functions, it has to be controlled in many instances if societies (and often, if individuals) are to survive. Societies use both internal and external control mechanisms. They are not equally effective in all situations.

Internal controls are those that exist within individuals and are related to a peoples' definitions of who they are. In other words, how people see themselves has much to do with their level of conformity. **External controls** come from outside of individuals. External control can be formal or informal. **Formal external controls** refers to the systems created by society specifically to control deviance, for example, courts, police officers, and prison. **Informal external controls** include sources of pressure from peers, friends, parents or other people whom one associates with, who apply pressure to encourage one to conform to the norms.

Journal instructions:
1. Attend a meeting of Alcoholics Anonymous or another group that counsels drug abusers.

2. Keep a detailed journal in which you record your observations of the meeting. Here are some things to look for during your observation:
   a) How is the meeting organized?
   b) How are newcomers socialized into the group?
   c) How are members encouraged to deal with their substance abuse problem?
   d) What methods does AA (or the group you are observing) use to help substance abusers?

3. Besides observing the meeting, interview one of the members or someone you know that is (or was) a member of AA or another group that counsels substance abusers. Ask them the above questions. In addition, ask them:
   a) Did the fact that particular drugs were illegal prevent you from using them?

b) What eventually led you to seek help from AA (or the group that you are in)?

4. After you conduct your observations and interviews, discuss in your journal the extent to which each type of social control — internal, external, formal, informal — was effective in helping curtail the AA members alcohol/drug problems.

5. Identify three occupations that deal with society's drug abuse problem and discuss how the knowledge of social control mechanisms might be useful in those occupations.

Option: essay
After you complete the above journal instructions, write an essay (around five to seven pages, typed) in which you discuss what you think the government's role should be in helping to curtail drug abuse. Base your discussion upon:
  a) the conclusions you reached in your journal about the effectiveness of different types of social control;
  b) various sociological theories of deviance (anomie theory, conflict theory, the social learning theories, and labeling theory). In other words, what might each of the theories of deviance offer that might be useful in dealing with society's drug abuse problem?

Option: research paper
Conduct library research to locate at least five to six articles from various sources (sociology journals, newspapers and magazines, commentary magazines, books, and so on) that can provide you with arguments for and against the legalization of controlled substances (marijuana, cocaine, LSD, "ecstasy," and so on). Be sure to find articles that present views that support and oppose legalization of drugs. Write a paper (around five to seven pages, typed) in which you:
  a) Explain and introduce what the issue of legalization is about.
  b) Carefully present strong arguments for and against drug legalization;
  c) Write a conclusion to your paper in which you use sociological theories about deviance and social control, and your journal observations and conclusions to elaborate your position either for or against legalization.

Be sure to provide proper documentation throughout your paper and include a reference page.

CHAPTER 8

Social Differentiation and Stratification

An important social issue that American society faces today is the growth of income inequality, commonly known as the gap between the rich and the poor. Consider the following facts compiled by the U.S. Congressional Office of Management and Budget:
• Between 1977 and 1990, the income for the richest fifth of American families increased thirty-four percent, but it decreased nine percent for the poorest fifth.
• The richest ten percent of Americans control over seventy percent of the wealth in this country.
• The richest one percent of Americans control over thirty percent of the wealth.

The growth of income inequality is an important sociological issue because it suggests that the nature of our system of ranking people in society is changing. In the past, while it may have been more difficult for some and easier for others to achieve a higher social and economic position, it was possible for most people to improve somewhat their overall lot in life. However, the extensive and persistent income inequality that exists in the United States today suggests that we may be becoming a society in which the chances for lower-income groups to achieve a higher social position are becoming less and less possible. This is significant because Americans have always emphasized a commitment to equality and a belief in the middle class life-style. The feasibility of maintaining that commitment may now be threatened.

ACTIVITY 8. 1

**How Has Your Family's Position In The Stratification System
Affected Your Life Chances, Opportunities,
And Development Of Self?**

Social stratification refers to the ranking of people based upon the amount of scarce resources - in industrial society, wealth, power, and prestige - they possess. Max Weber felt that in industrialized societies, there are three resources around which social stratification revolves: **social class, social status,** and **party.** These resources affect the nature of a stratification system and people's relationship to these resources affects their position in a stratification system.

According to Weber, a **social class** refers to a category of people who have approximately the same amount of power and wealth and the same life chances to acquire wealth.

Social status refers to the amount of honor and prestige a person receives from others in the community.

Parties are organizations in which decisions are made on how to reach important social goals.

Journal instructions:
1. Read the chapter about social stratification in your textbook, paying particular attention to the above concepts and the sections about the relationship between stratification and life chances. (If your text does not discuss stratification and life chances, there are a number of introductory texts that have good discussions on this topic. For example, Eshleman, Cashion, and Basirico, 1993; Eitzen and Baca Zinn, 1992; Thio, 1992; and many others. Look in your library or ask to borrow one from your sociology professor.)

2. Think about and list in your journal all of the ways in which peoples' positions in the stratification system can affect (positively or negatively) their life chances and opportunities (for example, housing, medical care, life expectancy, education, employment, mate selection, family stability, justice, and so on).

3. For each item in your list, write two or three sentences on how a person's class, status, and party can affect their life chances. Then comment briefly on how class, status, and party has affected <u>your</u> life.

57

4. Re-read the sections from the chapter on socialization in your introductory text about theories of socialization and the self. Use the theories about socialization and the self to think about and discuss (in your journal) how a person's life chances affect their socialization and sense of self. For example, how does being socialized in a school in an upper-middle class neighborhood where teachers may have high expectations of students affect a student's sense of self, motivation, ambition, self confidence, and so on? What about in a school in a lower class neighborhood? What might Cooley's "looking glass self" or Mead's "role taking" theories have to offer about this? And so on. Think of all the ways in which position in the stratification system affects the way we are socialized.

Option: essay
Write an essay (around five pages, typed) in which you discuss how <u>your</u> family's position in the stratification system has affected your life chances, your socialization, and your sense of self. In other words, discuss how your family's position in the stratification system has influenced who you are today.

Option: bibliography
1. Conduct library research on the topic of how stratification affects people's life chances and opportunities. Use key words, phrases, or ideas such as housing, educational attainment, family stability, life expectancy, and many others to search through your library's reference and resource material for articles and books about the effects of stratification on people's life chances and opportunities.

2. Generate a bibliography of fifteen to twenty articles (primarily from sociology journals) and books about the effects of different dimensions of stratification on people's life chances and opportunities. Type your bibliography using proper reference style. (See Activity 1. 3.)

Option: research paper
Write a paper (around seven pages, typed) in which you integrate your journal discussions and at least four items from your bibliography into a discussion about how <u>your</u> family's position in the stratification system has affected your life chances, your socialization, and your sense of self. You can use the bibliographic material in a variety of ways. For example, use it to help you explain how certain dimensions of stratification have affected your life; or you might use examples from your life to illustrate some of the ideas found in your library research material. Be sure to cite all of your bibliographic references properly in your paper, and include a reference (works cited) page.

ACTIVITY 8. 2

Observing How Stratification Affects Others' Life Chances

Journal instructions:
1. Identify and locate an upper-middle class neighborhood and a lower class neighborhood in the area in which you live or attend school.

2. By yourself or with one of your classmates, observe each neighborhood for two afternoons (around three hours each). Keep a journal in which you record your observations about everyday life in the neighborhoods. The following is a list of some items you can focus on, but do not feel limited to this list:
   a) the types and conditions of the houses;
   b) the types and conditions of the automobiles;
   c) the condition of the schools, inside and out;
   d) the condition of the public parks;
   e) the conditions of the roads;
   f) the types of stores, the condition they are in, the types of products that are available, and the quality of the products;
   g) the hospitals and medical facilities;
   h) the amount of police protection or police surveillance.

3. After you have completed your observations, use the theories, concepts, ideas, and research findings in your textbook's chapter on social stratification to discuss the impact of social class on people's life chances and opportunities in both communities that you observed.

Option: class presentation
Prepare a five- to ten-minute presentation to your class about your observations and conclusions.

ACTIVITY 8. 3

How Much Does It Cost To Live? Why Are The Poor Still Poor?

Surveys repeatedly show that most Americans regard the poor as being responsible for their own poverty and believe that people on welfare could find work if they really wanted to do so (Waxman, 1983). These, and other myths about the poor, are out of line with reality. Most poor people either work or cannot find jobs. Over twenty-five percent of poor people are working, but they earn too little to bring them out of poverty, yet too much to allow them to receive welfare subsidies(Giddens, 1991).

In 1990, the U.S. Government defined the poverty line at $12,675 annually for a family of four. Besides being an indicator of the number of people who are officially poor in the United States, this figure is one of the measures used to determine if people are eligible for particular forms of government assistance. Is this an accurate figure? Does this figure reflect what it really costs a family of four to live in today's society? Are people poor because they do not work hard enough?

Journal instructions:
1. Prepare a budget of expenses for a family of four to live in the city in which you currently reside. Proceed as follows:
   a) Make three columns on a sheet of paper in your journal or notebook.
   b) Label the first column, budget items. In this column, list all of the items that have to be paid for each month. These include, but are not limited to, the following: housing (rent or mortgage), utilities (gas, electric, water), telephone, medical care (office visits, drugs, insurance), food, clothing, transportation (car payments, insurance, or other transportation costs), education expenses for children, etc. Think about this list carefully and include any other items that should be on the list. You may want to ask your parents or someone who pays their family's bills for suggestions of what to include on this list.
   b) Label the second column, minimum monthly expense. In this column, estimate for each item in the first column what you think the absolute minimum monthly expense for that item would be. That is, what is the bare minimum that you think a family of four could spend on that item.
   c) Label the third column, projected monthly expense. In this column, take a more realistic approach. Estimate the expense that you think a family of four of which you are a member is <u>likely</u> to incur each month.

2. Using your monthly budget estimates, calculate the total annual expense. (That is, add up each column and multiply by twelve.) Based upon your budget estimates, these figures indicate the net income, that is, income after taxes are taken out, that a family of four needs to meet their minimum living expenses and your projected living expenses.

3. Considering these estimates, how appropriate is the government's figure for the poverty level?

4. How many full time, minimum wage jobs would it take to meet the needs of the budgets you estimated?

5. Based upon your budget, what would the minimum wage per hour have to be for one person to support a family of four? What would it have to be for two people to support a family of four?

6. In light of your findings, think about and discuss in your journal why people are poor. Are people poor, as most Americans believe, because they are not determined enough to work?

Option: essay
Write an essay (around three to five pages, typed) in which you use your journal material and theories of stratification (structural functional theory and conflict theory) to discuss why poverty persists in American society.

ACTIVITY 8. 4

Do The Wealthy Pay Their Fair Share Of Taxes?

As discussed in the introduction to this chapter, the income gap between the rich and poor has increased significantly during the last decade. Many argue that this is partially because during this same period the wealthy paid a lower rate of taxation than the middle and lower classes. In other words, a policy of progressive taxation has not been enforced.

Progressive taxation means that the rate of tax that people pay will increase as their income goes up and will decrease as their income goes down. While progressive taxation has always been the official national tax policy of the United States, various types of loopholes and tax breaks have led to a system in which progressive taxation does not necessarily exist.

Journal instructions:
1. Obtain and read "A Far Cry From Fair: CTJ's Guide to State Tax Reform" (McIntyre et al., 1991). Ask your librarian if your library has a copy, or order it (or ask your library to order it) from Citizens for Tax Justice, 1311 L Street, NW, Washington, D.C. 20005. Telephone: (202) 626-3780. It is free of charge.

2. In your journal discuss the rates of taxation—as indicated in the CTJ Guide—for different income groups in the state in which you live and for five other states. Which income groups pay the highest and the lowest rates? Does this seem fair to you? Why or why not?

Option: essay (letter to the editor of a local newspaper or your congressperson)
Write an opinion essay or a letter to the editor of your local newspaper, or a letter to your congressperson, in which you espouse your viewpoint about taxes. Use the information you obtained and developed in your journal (above) as the basis of your letter. Remember that you are writing to an

61

audience that is not familiar with sociological terms, so present your discussion in a way that it can be understood.

Option: research paper

1. Conduct library research about progressive taxation in the United States. Use the library's indexes and catalogues to help you find at least four sources (for example, Eshleman, Cashion, and Basirico, 1993; Phillips, 1990; Kinsley 1990; Reich, 1991; Maxwell, 1990; Ehrenreich, 1990; and many others) that will help you address the following:
   a) the extent to which progressive taxation exists;
   b) arguments for stricter progressive tax;
   c) arguments against progressive taxation;
   d) data about tax rates and income levels.

Use government documents (ask you librarian for suggestions) or locate an article in a periodical that summarizes some of these data.

2. Write a paper (around five to seven pages, typed) in which you use your library research and journal discussion (above) to:
   a) discuss the extent to which progressive taxation exists in the United States at the federal and state levels;
   b) discuss at least three reasons for enacting stricter progressive taxation policies and at least three reasons against enacting stricter policies.
   c) use structural functional theory, conflict theory, and other material in your introductory text's chapter on social stratification to evaluate the arguments for and against strict progressive taxation.

ACTIVITY 8. 5

How Much Social Mobility Has Occurred In Your Family?

Vertical social mobility—changing social positions upward or downward—is influenced by a number of factors. Sociologists often look at two types of vertical social mobility: **intergenerational mobility** and **intragenerational mobility**.

Intergenerational mobility refers to the changes upward or downward in class or status between generations, say, from your grandparents to your parents to yourself. **Intragenerational mobility** refers to the changes upward or downward within your own lifetime.

Journal instructions:
1. Read the section on social mobility in the chapter on social stratification in your introductory text. In your journal, identify and explain the following:

a) the structural factors that can affect social mobility;
b) individual factors that can affect social mobility;
c) the way in which opportunities and life chances affect social mobility.

2. In your journal, use the information that you compiled above to trace, discuss, and analyze the intergenerational mobility within your family for at least the last two generations previous to yours (that is, from your grandparents to your parents). If possible, go back to your great grandparents' generation. Additionally, trace and analyze the extent of intragenerational mobility that the current family in which you live has experienced.

Option: essay
1. Write an essay (around five pages, typed) in which you analyze the intergenerational and intragenerational mobility within your family as discussed in your journal. Structure your essay around the following items:
a) the various structural factors that affected your family's mobility during different generations and time periods;
b) how the dimensions of stratification (class, status, party) have affected your family's mobility;
c) how individual factors affected your family's mobility.

2. Based upon your family's social mobility, conclude your essay with a discussion of the relevance of structural functional theory of stratification and conflict theory of stratification. Based upon your family's experience, which do you feel is the more appropriate explanation of inequality in the United States?

ACTIVITY 8. 6

The Relationship Between Sociological Theories of Stratification and Political Viewpoints

The sociological theories of stratification - structural functional theory and conflict theory - are two very different views about the nature of stratification systems and explanations about why inequality exists. Practical applications of these theories seem to exist within the American politics. Although the political views of Republicans, Democrats, conservatives and liberals are not necessarily based upon structural functional theory and conflict theory, there does seem to be some similarity between the political views and the sociological theories.

Journal instructions:
1. Review the sections in the chapter on social stratification in your introductory text about the structural functional and conflict theories of stratification. Summarize the major ideas of each in your journal.

2. Interview a political science professor at your college and/or a local, state, or federal politician. Record their responses in your journal.
   a) Explain the structural functional and conflict theories of stratification to the person you interview.
   b) Ask the person how each of these theories relates or compares to the views of the Democratic and Republican parties and to conservative and liberal political views.
   c) Ask the person for an example of an issue related to economic or social inequality in which Republicans and Democrats, or conservatives and liberals, have deeply divided views (for example, taxes, funding for education, minimum wage, health care or others).

3. In your journal, discuss some parallels between the political views (Republican vs. Democrat, conservative vs. liberal) and sociological theories of stratification (structural functionalism vs. conflict theory).

Option: research paper
1. Use your library's indexes (for example, *Reader's Guide to Periodical Literature, Social Science Index, Newsbank, New York Times Index,* or other indexes) to locate four to six articles or documents (political speeches, contents of political debates, and so on) about the issue you discussed with the person you interviewed. Obtain the right combination of articles to provide you with the various political views about the issue in question. Read the articles and look for parallels between the contrasting political views on the issue and the sociological theories of stratification (structural functional and conflict theory).

2. Based upon your library research and your journal, write an essay (around five pages, typed) in which you compare sociological theories of stratification with the political views. Be sure to:
   a) Discuss the relationship between the sociological theories and the political views. That is, which political views are similar to which sociological theories and how?
   b) Illustrate this relationship by discussing the position that each political view has with regard to the particular social issue you discussed with the political science professor or politician.
   c) Illustrate your points with quotes and excerpts from your library research. Be sure to cite all references properly and include a reference (works cited) page.

CHAPTER 9

Racial and Ethnic Differentiation

The history of race and ethnic relations in the United States has been marked by conflict, competition, prejudice, and discrimination. Ethnic and racial inequality continues to exist to a large extent in American society. Most ethnic and racial minority groups in the United States lag far behind European-Americans in terms of median family incomes (Currie and Skolnick, 1988). Native-Americans, African-Americans, and Hispanic-Americans are much more likely than European-Americans to be unemployed, sporadically employed, or underemployed; thus, they are more likely to occupy positions with the lowest income, benefits, security, and status (Neubeck, 1991). Minorities are also more likely to be be illiterate and are less likely to complete high school and to go to college. Additionally, nonwhite families are more likely to experience a divorce and are more likely to be headed by single women than white families.

The riots in Los Angeles that lasted for a week in spring of 1992—triggered when the white police officers taped beating black motorist Rodney King were acquitted—provided very strong evidence that American society is still experiencing tumultuous race relations. While riots are not everyday expressions of the racial and ethnic tensions in the United States, much of African-American popular culture—for example, rap music and films about inner-city experiences—is evidence that many African-Americans are still highly perturbed about the growing economic and social inequality between white and non-white Americans.

Besides the occasional riots and expressions of popular culture, scholars widely agree that racial and ethnic inequality in America exists. The statistical evidence is overwhelming. What they disagree about is *why* racial and ethnic groups suffer from so much inequality.

ACTIVITY 9. 1

How Has Racial and Ethnic Group Membership Affected Your Life?

As does our position in the stratification system, our racial and ethnic group membership affects our life chances and who we are. Whether or not we are members of a minority group, all of us have been affected—positively or negatively—by the differential treatment of racial and ethnic minorities. Our world views, perspectives, statuses, roles, norms, beliefs, values and life chances have been very much affected—sometimes determined—by the social forces surrounding race, ethnicity, and minority status.

Journal instructions:
1. Go to your introductory sociology text and read about discrimination and prejudice. In your journal, list and briefly discuss the ways in which you or members of your family personally have ever experienced ethnic or racial discrimination or prejudice. For example, on the sole basis of your race or ethnicity: Have you ever been the object of slurs? Has anyone ever feared you? Has anyone ever attributed particular traits (positive or negative) to you? Have your ever been denied or given opportunities? And so on. In other words, have you or your family members ever been prejudged and acted toward—positively or negatively—primarily on the basis of your racial or ethnic group membership?

2. List and briefly discuss the ways in which you or members of your family have ever expressed ethnic or racial prejudice or discrimination.

3. Reread the following sections in your introductory text and make comments in your journal about the ways in which material from these readings (concepts, theories, research findings, and so on) apply to things you discussed above:
   a) In the chapter on racial and ethnic minorities, read about how life chances are influenced by race and ethnicity.
   b) In the chapter on social stratification, read about how life chances are influenced by social class.
   c) In the chapter on socialization, read about theories of socialization and the self.

Option: essay
Write an essay (around five to seven pages, typed) in which you discuss how your life (opportunities, life chances, perspectives, sense of self, and so on) has been influenced by your racial or ethnic group affiliation. Be sure to use specific examples from your journal and apply specific theories, ideas, concepts, and so on from your sociology text.

Option: research paper

1. Conduct library research to find four or five relevant books or articles (preferably from sociology journals, but not necessarily) about the effects of race or ethnicity on various aspects of people's life chances and sense of self. (For example, you might find research articles or books on discrimination, prejudice, income, education, health care, socialization, and so on in terms of race and ethnicity.)

2. Use your library research and your journal to write a paper (around five to seven pages, typed) in which you discuss how your life, and your sense of self, has been influenced by your racial or ethnic group affiliation. Be sure to provide proper documentation throughout your paper and include a reference page.

ACTIVITY 9. 2

Does Fair Housing Exist In Your Neighborhood?

In the United States, housing discrimination on the basis of age, gender, race, ethnicity, religion, physical disability, or type of family is against the law. Fair housing—that is, equal opportunity in finding a dwelling—has been mandated by the Title VIII of the Civil Rights Act of 1968 (commonly known as the Fair Housing Law) and subsequent amendments. Yet, five types of housing discrimination are still prevalent in the United States, even though prohibited by law:

Steering—when a real estate broker directs or "steers" minority group clients away from white areas, and steers white clients away from neighborhoods occupied by racial or ethnic minorities.

Intimidation—a type of steering in which a real estate broker warns, or "intimidates" clients by telling them, perhaps sincerely, that they probably would not be happy living in a certain neighborhood because the residents there are prejudiced against minorities.

Misrepresentation—when minority clients are told that the property they are interested in has been sold when in fact it has been not, or the price has been artificially raised beyond the clients' reach.

Blockbusting—when homeowners real estate agents or developers try to frighten homeowners into selling their homes at an artificially low price by telling them that minorities are moving into their neighborhood and that as a result they may have trouble selling their home at a future date.

67

Redlining—when mortgage lenders or insurance companies make it difficult or impossible for people to obtain a mortgage or insurance in racially or ethnically mixed areas.

Although instances of housing discrimination are difficult to prove, it is likely that you know someone that has been either a victim or a perpetrator.

Journal instructions:
1. Interview five non-white Americans and five white Americans who rent or own a home (house, apartment, condominium) and record their responses in your journal:
    a) Explain the above types of discrimination to each of them.
    b) Ask each of them if they, or anybody they know, has ever been a victim of any of these types of discrimination (either for renting or buying a home). If yes, ask them to explain.
    c) Ask each of them if there are any conditions under which they would refuse to rent or sell their real estate property (apartment, condominium, or house) to someone. If so, ask them to explain.

2. In your journal, compare the responses given by whites and non-whites whom you interviewed.

3. Ask your librarian if the library has any documents from the U.S. Department of Housing and Urban Development (HUD) and/or the Department of Human Relations in your state. If not, contact the HUD office nearest to the city in which you live and/or the Human Relations Council in your state. The telephone number is available from your local operator or ask your reference librarian for assistance in obtaining the telephone number. Once you contact either of the above offices, ask to speak to someone who could provide you with information about the extent to which housing discrimination has been reported in your state and in the city in which you live. Tell the person that you would like to obtain any documents that provide information about the extent of housing discrimination in the state and city in which you live.

4. Once you obtain the documents, examine them. In your journal, discuss the following:
    a) What types of information do they provide about discrimination?
    b) What do they tell you about the extent to which housing discrimination exists in the state and in city where you live.
    c) Identify two or three occupations that you feel could use this type of information.
    d) Is there more or less discrimination occuring in your state than you thought?

e) Using theories of discrimination found within the chapter on racial and ethnic minorities in your introductory text, explain why you think the level of housing discrimination in your state and in your city is as high or as low as it is.

Option: class presentation
Prepare a five- to ten-minute presentation to your class in which you discuss the material you collected and explored in your journal.

ACTIVITY 9. 3

Stereotypes, Prejudice, and Discrimination

We all are members of ethnic and racial groups. Each of us, whether we like it or not, hold particular **stereotypes** of people in ethnic and racial groups. And, as members of ethnic and racial groups, others hold stereotypes of us. Stereotypes can lead to **prejudice** and **discrimination.** Read about these concepts in your introductory sociology text.

Journal instructions:
1. For one week, keep an extensive journal in which you record racial and ethnic stereotypes and prejudices that you observe, hear, witness, express personally, or are the object of. These can occur anywhere: interactions between friends, in your family, by teachers or students in or out of the classroom, on television programs, in advertisements, in newspapers, magazines, on MTV, and so on.

2. In your journal, describe each of your observations of racial or ethnic stereotypes or prejudices.

3. On what basis (for example, myth, personal experience, and so on) do you think each of these stereotypes or prejudices was made?

4. Using theories of prejudice and discrimination that you read about in your text, discuss some reasons for the prejudice that you observed.

5. Discuss some dysfunctions (negative consequences) of each of the stereotypes and prejudices that you observe. For example, what types of discrimination and blocked opportunities might occur as a result?

Option: essay
Write an essay (around five pages, typed) in which you use the observations from your journal to discuss how prejudice in everyday life and its consequences.

ACTIVITY 9. 4

Institutionalized Racism and Discrimination

Institutionalized discrimination is the continuing exclusion or oppression of a group as a result of criteria established by an institution or community. Individual prejudice is not a factor, and laws or rules are not necessarily <u>intentionally</u> applied to prevent people of a certain race or ethnic group from belonging. However, the result is that one group is systematically denied access to membership in the larger group or community.

Similarly, **institutionalized racism** is when racist ideas and practices are built in to the folkways, mores, or laws of an institution or community. Reread the sections about institutionalized discrimination and racism in the chapter on racial and ethnic groups in your introductory text.

Journal instructions:
1. Identify four situations or organizations in your community where it might be **possible** for institutionalized discrimination or racism to take place (for example, colleges, country clubs, other types of private clubs, campus groups such as fraternities or sororities, exclusive housing developments, and so on.)

2. In your journal, speculate and discuss how institutionalized discrimination or racism might occur in such situations or organizations.

3. Examine the admission criteria or policies of two of these organizations or situations. There are a number of ways that you can find out this information. Here are some examples, but do not feel limited to these:
   a) Call or visit a private country club in your area. Ask to speak to the person who is in charge of membership. Once you contact the appropriate person, tell him or her that you are interested in obtaining an application and information for a friend who is moving into the area about how to become a member of the club.
   b) Find out the criteria that the various fraternities and sororities at your college have for become a pledge. You can obtain this information directly from the Greek organization itself, or ask the office of student affairs how you can obtain this information.
   c) Ask a local real estate agent about the new housing developments in your area. Ask them to provide you with the criteria necessary for building a house in that area (for example, size of lot, size of house, and so on).

3. Once you obtain the criteria for membership in the organizations you selected, read them carefully. Are there any groups that are likely to be

excluded or deterred from joining or seeking membership because of some of the criteria for membership? Explain.

ACTIVITY 9. 5

Patterns of Ethnic and Racial Group Interaction Where You Live

There are a number of patterns that can occur when various ethnic and racial groups reside in the same area. These can be represented by 3 models.

One model is referred to as **assimilation** or **Anglo-conformity** and is often represented as: A + B + C = A. Here, A refers to the dominant Anglo-American - that is, WASP (White Anglo-Saxon Protestant) - culture. In this model, other racial and ethnic groups become integrated into the dominant culture by forsaking their own cultural traditions and adopting the Anglo-American traditions.

A second model is referred to as **the melting pot** or **amalgamation** and is often represented as: A + B + C = D. Here, racial and ethnic cultures mix to form new cultural traditions, with some elements of each, but distinct from any one of them.

A third model is referred to as **cultural pluralism** or **multiculturalism** and is often represented as: A + B + C = A + B + C. In this model, the culture of each racial and ethnic group is recognized as equally valid and practiced in the society.

Read about the above patterns of racial and ethnic interaction in your introductory text.

Journal instructions:
1. Using census information, determine the extent to which the racial and ethnic population for the city in which you live has changed during the last decade. For example, how did the percentage of whites, blacks, Hispanics, Asians, and so on, change within your city? Compile these data and discuss the following items in your journal.

2. In addition to looking at the whole city, look at the racial and ethnic composition for each census tract within the city. Make a list of the census tracts and indicate the percent of the total population that is white, black, Hispanic, and so on.

3. Discuss how the the information you collected from the census reflects any of the patterns of interaction described in the chapter on ethnic and racial groups in your introductory text.

4. Consider which model of racial and ethnic patterns (above) best represents racial and ethnic relations in your city. Discuss some things you could observe that would help you determine the pattern that exists currently and what the future might look like. For example, what could you find out about each of the following in order to help you determine the pattern of racial and ethnic relations in your city: schools, churches, political representation, stores, mutual aid groups, community organizations, recreation centers, parks, and so on? Are there other clues you could look for?

5. Think about and discuss how knowledge of racial and ethnic patterns could be useful for people in five different occupations (for example, businesspeople, journalists, teachers, politicians, builders, real estate agents, city planners, and so on).

Option: essay
Write an essay (around three to five pages, typed) in which you discuss the type of ethnic and racial patterns that exist within your city.

Option: essay
1. Think about some things you could observe to assess the type of racial and ethnic patterns that exist at your college. Here are some examples, but do not confine yourself only to these:
   a) Attend meetings of different racial and ethnic organizations (for example, the Black Cultural Society, the Italian Club, and so on).
   b) Interview members of various ethnic and racial groups and discuss with them if they think the campus follows the assimilation, melting pot, or multicultural models.
   c) Observe patterns of interaction. Do members of the same racial or ethnic groups tend to sit together in classrooms and in the cafeteria? Do they tend to congregate together at other places on campus?
   d) Are there separate residence halls or floors for members of different ethnic and racial groups?
   e) Do racial and ethnic group members have their own fraternities, sororities, and other organizations?

2. Write an essay (around five pages, typed) in which you discuss the racial and ethnic group patterns of interaction at your college. Be sure to base your essay on the types of patterns discussed in your introductory text.

CHAPTER 10

Gender Differentiation

The majority of women today are in the work force. Nearly fifty percent of the work force consists of women. As of 1990, though, women earned only seventy-one cents for every dollar men earned (up from 61 cents in the mid-1970s—an increase of only ten cents in two decades). At the highest ranks of employment the situation is worse. In 1990, women held less than one half percent of most senior management jobs. Within these jobs, women's earnings were sixty-seven cents for every dollar paid to a man. Women with the title of vice president earned only fifty-eight cents to every dollar earned by a man. These figures suggest that while more women are entering the work force, inequality between men and women increases the further up the career ladder you look.

Regardless of what most women are doing, women and men are still perceived in terms of stereotypical traditional gender roles. Traditional prejudices and stereotypes about gender roles—the perception of what women and men *should* do, of who is responsible for supporting the family and who is responsible for raising it, of who is better at particular jobs in the work place, and so on—are partially responsible for the continuation of economic and political policies that keep women from achieving equality with men.

ACTIVITY 10. 1

Gender Roles And Social Policy

A major theme of the 1992 presidential election was "The Year of the Woman." While this theme is not unprecedented in major political campaigns, a consideration of women's role in society seems to be more evident than ever before in the political arena. One reason for this is that women's—and, consequently, men's—changing roles in society, especially in the workplace and in the family, have led to the need for political representation that can help women achieve equality in the workplace and other areas of social life. Economic and political policies regarding family leave, child care, reproductive rights, sexual discrimination, sexual harassment, the Equal Rights Amendment, and others are some of the major issues that politicians concerned with gender equality have said need to be addressed.

Journal instructions:

1. Look through back issues of national and local newspapers for the previous one to two years. Locate fifteen to twenty news articles, essays, letters to the editor, and so forth that address various policies related to women's issues. (See the introduction to this activity for suggestions.) Try to get a representation of different policy issues and diverse viewpoints on these issues.

2. Keep a record of the news items (articles, essays, letters to the editor, etc.) in your journal. You may want to photo copy each and keep them in your journal, or summarize each, indicating the newspaper, date, and page.

3. List each of the policy issues in your journal and briefly summarize what the various positions (that is, views) regarding each one are. (For example, what are the various positions regarding the reproductive rights of women, national child care policies, family leave policies, and so on?)

4. Discuss the assumptions about gender roles that are contained with the various positions about the policy. For example, what are the assumptions about gender roles in a position that supports enough child care resources to allow both parents to work full-time outside the home? What are the assumptions about gender roles in a position that does not support enough child care resources to allow both parents to work full-time?

5. Select one of the above policy issues that you identified. Interview an activist (for example, a community leader, politician, clergyperson, and so on) who supports the policy and one who opposes the policy. Ask the person to provide you with solid reasons for the position he or she takes. In addition, ask the person to explain his or her views about women's and men's respective roles in society, especially with regard to the family.

Option: research paper

1. Conduct library research on the topic that you chose. Obtain at least four to six references (newspaper and magazine articles, journal articles, books, and so on) about the topic. Be sure that you obtain references that can provide you with at least three arguments for and three arguments against the policy.

2. Write a short paper (around five pages, typed) in which you present a policy debate for and against a particular issue that concerns women primarily. In your debate, be sure to include a discussion of the implicit and explicit assumptions about gender roles that underlie each position in the debate. Be sure to provide proper documentation of your references throughout your paper, and include a reference (works cited) page.

ACTIVITY 10. 2

Bases Of Gender Differentiation

The nature vs. nurture debate about the development of human beings also exists with regard to explanations of gender differences. Clearly, there are differences in behavioral expectations for males and females (**gender roles**). Some studies have found that males and females tend to have different emotional, physical, and cognitive skills (cf. eg, Macoby and Jacklin, 1974). However, it is not clear whether these are due to differences in biological traits or to differences in socialization. While males and females are different biologically, sociologists generally believe that social factors are responsible for differences in behavior and equality among the genders (Nielsen, 1990). For example, biologically, women tend to have greater finger dexterity than men; yet, at least in the United States, most dentists and surgeons are men. Why? Cross-cultural studies show that the variety of gender roles men and women play in societies depends on the norms of the society and not on any physical characteristics.

Journal instructions:
1. Reread the sections in your introductory text about the ways in which people develop their gender identities and learn their gender roles. These sections will most likely appear in your introductory textbook's chapter on socialization or gender or both.

2. In your journal, make a list of the ways in which socialization into gender identity and gender roles takes place (family, media, religion, education, peers, interaction, and so on).

3. Imagine that you are observing gender roles in American society (or any other, for that matter) with "fresh eyes," that is, as if for the first time. You want to find out if males and females, as children and adults, are socialized (or taught or encouraged) to adopt particular types of identities and roles related to their respective gender. Develop a plan in which you observe a different setting in which gender identity and gender role socialization might occur for one hour per day, everyday for one week. Proceed as follows:

a) Identify seven possible settings you might observe (one for each day of the week). There are innumerable possibilities. For example, a religious service (for children or adults), a nursery school or day care center, a toy store, a playground, children's or adult television programs, television commercials, children's books, magazines, advertisements, employment settings, children's bedrooms, and so on. Be creative.

b) Once you identify the seven settings, make a list of things that you would look for in each setting. For example, in a toy store you might look at how the toys are arranged. Are there some toys that are clearly intended as "boy" toys and "girl" toys? What indicates that toys are separated according to gender? Is it the packaging, who appears on a box, the colors, and so on? Are there some toys that are clearly intended for both? What do the sales people recommend for boys and girls? (You might ask a salesperson what they would suggest as a gift for your three year-old niece or nephew.) And so on. There are many other clues that you can look for that might suggest gender role socialization. Do this for each of the seven settings you identified.

4. Now that you have your list of settings and things to observe, develop a plan for one week (around your class, extracurricular, and work schedule) in which you could observe a different setting every day for one hour per day. For example, on Sunday you might observe a religious service, on Tuesday you might observe a toy store, on Wednesday you might observe a child care center, and so on. Be sure to take detailed and careful notes in your journal during your observation of each setting. In addition, immediately after your observation, spend a few minutes writing down some comments about what you observed, your interpretations, conclusion, ideas, and so on.

Option: essay
At the tend of the week, review your journal and write a short paper (about five pages) in which you discuss why and how you developed your research plan and what some of your conclusions are about the biological and sociological bases of gender differentiation. Summarize what you found from your observations and interpret them in terms of the material in your introductory textbook's chapters on socialization, gender roles, and gender differentiation.

Option: research paper
Conduct library research to find around four articles from sociology journals that address some of the types of situations you observed (for example, gender role socialization in education, family, media, popular culture, religion, and so on). Write a paper (around five to seven pages, typed) in which you integrate the findings from your library research and your journal to discuss sociological bases of gender differentiation. Be sure to provide proper documentation throughout your paper and include a reference page.

ACTIVITY 10. 3

Gender Differentiation In The Workplace

As mentioned in the introduction to this chapter, gender inequality in the workplace is still a very real issue. Besides the wage gap between men and women, other factors such as **the glass ceiling, mommy tracks, a split labor market**, and others help to perpetuate inequality in the work place. The **glass ceiling** refers to the barrier that enables women to glimpse the upper management positions, but not attain them because of male traditions, prejudices, and stereotypes of women. **Mommy tracks** refers to employment situations in which women who choose to integrate family responsibilities into their schedules may have to sacrifice professional advancement. The **split labor market** means that there are two distinct and unequal groups of workers. The **primary labor market** is reserved for people—most often men —who will advance to high-level positions. The **secondary labor market**— sometimes referred to by sociologists as *women's ghettos*—are the subordinate jobs that contain little, if any, chance of professional advancement. The purpose of this activity is to have you examine the extent to which gender differentiation exists in the workplace and to consider why.

Journal instructions:
1. Make a list of all of the types of employment that exist at your college (secretaries, administrators, registrars, clerks, professors, groundkeepers, cafeteria workers, receptionists, and so on). Proceed as follows:
  a) Obtain a copy of the college catalogue. (If your college catalogue does not have such a list, ask the human resources administrator or secretary at your school if a list is available. It shouldn't take you more than thirty minutes to an hour to obtain the information you need from it.)
  b) In the back of the catalogue you will probably find a list of all of the personnel at the college (their names, position, and other relevant information). Read through the list of personnel in order, and keep a list of each different type of employment.
  c) As you read through the list, keep a tally of the number of men and the number of women in each employment position. (You should be able to tell by their names.) Keep a record of how many men and how many women are in each position.
  d) Then calculate the percentage of women and men that do each particular job. (For example, ninety-five percent of the secretaries are female, five percent are men; eighty-five percent of the administrators are male, fifteen percent are women; and so on for each position.)
  e) In addition, find out the number of members on the Board of Trustees, what percentage are men, and what percentage are women?

2. After you complete your list, observe someone who works in <u>each</u> of those positions (excluding the Board of Trustees). Briefly describe in your journal what they do, the difficulty of their job, and the likelihood for professional advancement (that is, moving to a higher position).

3. Rank the jobs in terms of what you think the salaries are, from highest to lowest. You do not have to come up with an actual number, simply rank the jobs. (For example, president, vice presidents, deans, professors, associate professors, assistant professors, secretaries, cashiers, and so on).

4. Divide the jobs into two lists: primary market and secondary market. What percent of the employees in each market are female and what percentage are male?

5. Interview a woman at your college who is an administrator (department chair, dean, vice president, human resources officer, registrar, and so on) and one who is a member of the faculty. In your journal, write down her answers to the following questions:
   a) Do men and women in the primary labor market at the school (mention the jobs you have in your primary market list) have the same chances for professional advancement at this college?
   b) Are there male traditions, stereotypes, or prejudices of women that still exist at the college—either overtly or covertly—that impede the advancement of women at the college? If so, what are they?
   c) Are there any ways in which women are denied the same opportunities for advancement as men —again, either overtly or covertly?

Option: essay
1. Reread the section on inequality in the workplace in the chapter on gender differentiation (stratification, inequality) in your introductory text.

2. Write an essay (around five pages, typed) in which you discuss the extent to which gender differentiation among employees exists at your school. Use the material that you compiled in your journal and analyze it with concepts, theories, and ideas contained in your text about gender differentiation in the workplace. Does it exist? To what extent? Why? What are the consequences?

ACTIVITY 10. 4

Is Household Equality Between Men And Women Increasing?

As Kathleen Gerson (1992) has noted, the breadwinner-homemaker household - that is, the family in which the male is the prime breadwinner and the female is the homemaker and caretaker of the children - continues to decline numerically and as a cultural ideal. Yet, even while most women are now in the labor force, women still spend more time on housework and childrearing than husbands, even when both are employed full-time.

The following are a few typical situations in which parents in almost every family with children often find themselves: a pediatrician's office, a children's dentist's office, a PTA meeting, a school bus stop, a drop-off and pick-up area outside an elementary or middle school for children whose parents drive them, a child-care center early in the morning when children are being dropped off and at pick-up time, a grocery store, a playground, an afternoon elementary school program, and an afternoon children's sporting event. Observing these situations can give us some clues as to who is caring for the household and children in our community.

Journal instructions:
1. Observe six or seven of the above situations (or come up with your own) for around thirty minutes to an hour <u>each</u> and note how many men and how many women are caring for their children, or performing household or childrearing duties. Record your observations in your journal.

2. Think about the types of duties and responsibilities that have to be fulfilled by husbands and wives, for example, buying the food, preparing meals, washing the dishes, earning income, paying bills, fixing things around the house, and many others. Make a list of these items in your journal. (Ask your parents for some suggestions as to what to include on this list.) Then compare the way in which these responsibilities are, have been, or will be met in three generations of your family: how they will likely be carried out in your family when you get married (or, if you are already married, how are they fulfilled now), the family you were raised in, and the family in which your parents were raised in (that is, your grandparents). If possible, discuss this with your parents and grandparents. In your journal, discuss why the duties and responsibilities in these families are/were distributed between the males and females.

Option: essay
Using your journal observations, write an essay (around three to five pages, typed) in which you discuss which household and child rearing responsibilities are being fulfilled by males and females, and whether or not these responsibilities are shifting. Analyze family gender roles from various theoretical perspectives (such as structural functionalism, conflict theory, symbolic interactionism, and exchange theory).

Option: research paper
Conduct library research in order to find four articles in sociology journals and books about gender equality in the family (eg., Gerson, 1992; Goldscheider and Waite, 1991; DeVault, 1991, and others). Write a paper (around five to seven pages, typed) in which you integrate ideas and findings from those articles with your journal material to discuss gender equality in the family. Be sure to document your references throughout the paper and include a reference (works cited) page.

ACTIVITY 10. 5

Women's Issues

As women become more politically active and as their role in the workplace continues to become more visible in American society, it is becoming clear that women are affected differently by different issues and have a different perspective than men on many issues. Because the United States has been a male-dominated society, the male perspective often has been portrayed as the norm. Thus, the legitimacy of women's points of view have been denied and often portrayed as deviant. The purpose of this activity is to help you become aware of issues from a feminist perspective.

Journal instructions:
1. Be an observer at three meetings of a "women's group." You can probably find one on your campus or in your community.

2. In your journal, keep a list of the issues and topics that the women discuss at their meeting. Write down comments about the issues that women talk about, what they face in everyday life, important political issues, and so on.

3. Interview one or two of the women present. Ask them what they feel some of the most important issues regarding women in society today are and why they are important.

4. Think of four occupations in which knowledge of women's issues and perspectives is important. How could this type of knowledge be useful in those occupations?

Option: class presentation
Complete the above journal instructions. Then, prepare a five- to ten-minute presentation for your class in which you discuss your observations of the women's group and occupations in which knowledge of women's issues is important.

CHAPTER 11

Age Differentiation and the Aged

The proportion of elderly as compared to the rest of the population in the United States has been growing since 1900 and it is expected to keep growing for the foreseeable future. In 1900, 3.1 million people, composing 4 percent of the population, were 65 years of age and older in the United States. In 1990, 31.8 million people, composing 12.7 percent of the population, were 65 years of age and older (*Statistical Abstract*, 1991:16). If current projections hold true—and there is no reason that they shouldn't since they are based upon the number of people alive today —the number of elderly will increase to around 66.5 million, or 21.5 percent of the population, by the year 2040—just around the time when today's 20 year-olds will be elderly. If you are around 20 years of age today, more than 1 in 5 people will be elderly when you are. Compare that to 1 in 12 who are elderly today.

There are many sociological issues related to the elderly that need to be considered such as employment, leisure, health, housing, family life, social security, and so on. How does the continuous increase in number and proportion of the elderly determine the types of issues and policies that society must address? What is the effect on the labor force, on social security, the economy, health care, politics, the family, the military, and other social institutions? What types of issues do the elderly themselves face in everyday life?

ACTIVITY 11. 1

Myths About Old Age

Sociological research about the elderly (a field of study known as **gerontology**) has debunked many myths. Some of the myths proven to be false are that old people predominantly tend to be: senile, unhappy, unhealthy, crime victims, poor, unable to manage a household, uninterested in sex, incapable of having sex, living in nursing homes and other institutions, unproductive, and set in their ways (Palmore, 1977; Kart, 1981). Gerontological research has found that these stereotypes of the elderly are false. Of course, some old people are senile, unhappy, unhealthy and so on. But so are some young people. Categorically attributing these characteristics to people on the basis of their age can lead to prejudice and discrimination (**ageism**) just as categorically attributing characteristics to people based upon their ethnicity, race, or gender.

Go to your introductory sociology text and study the sections about stereotypes, prejudice, and discrimination in the chapters on racial and ethnic groups, in the chapter on gender, and in the chapter on aging.

Journal instructions:
1. For one week, keep an extensive journal in which you record your observations of stereotypes and prejudices toward the elderly. How are they portrayed in television programs and commercials? How are they talked about among your friends? How are they portrayed in movies? How are they portrayed in newspaper and magazine advertisements? And so forth.

2. What myth(s) is each stereotype and prejudice based upon and what myth(s) do they reinforce?

3. Discuss some dysfunctions (negative consequences) of each of the stereotypes and prejudices that you observed?

4. Interview at least five people over sixty-five years of age (no more than one from your family).
   a) Present the above list of myths about the elderly to them. Share with them some of your observations for the week. Ask them to discuss with you the extent to which these myths are generally true.
   b) Ask them if they or any of their friends or relatives have ever been the target of prejudice or discrimination because of their elderly status. If so, ask them to explain.
   c) Ask them if they think the prejudice or discrimination was justified.
   d) Ask them what the effect of the prejudice or discrimination was on their, or their friends', lives. For example: Did they lose a job? Were they denied a job or opportunity? Did it affect their sense of self? Did it affect their relationships with others? And so forth.

Option: class presentation
Summarize your journal findings and discuss them, and any conclusions you arrived at, with your class in a five- to ten-minute presentation.

Option: essay

1.   Which theories or explanations of stereotypes, prejudice, and discrimination of minority groups (see relevant chapters in your text) can be used to explain stereotypes and prejudices toward the elderly? What are the ways in which institutional discrimination of the elderly can occur?

2.   Write an essay (around five pages, typed) in which you analyze (based upon your journal observations and interviews) the types of stereotypes, prejudice, and discrimination against the elderly that occur in everyday life. In your essay:

   a) Discuss stereotypes, prejudices, and discrimination that you discovered through your observations and interviews. Using examples, discuss the myths they are based upon and the dysfunctions for the elderly.

   b) Using appropriate theories of prejudice and discrimination that you read about in various chapters of your introductory text, explain why prejudice and discrimination of the elderly occurs. Compare similarities and differences of ageism with racism and sexism.

Option: essay

Watch three or four episodes of the television program *The Golden Girls*. Using specific examples from the show, write an essay (around three to five pages, typed) in which you discuss how the themes and the humor in the program are based upon various myths about the elderly.

Option: essay

Watch the movie *Harold and Maude* (1971). It is available on VHS at most rental video stores and possibly in your college's library. Write an essay (around five pages, typed) in which you discuss how stereotypes and myths about age form the basis for much of the humor in this movie.

ACTIVITY 11. 2

Using Sociological Theories To Examine Social Issues About The Elderly

Gerontology has become one of the most rapidly-growing areas of sociology. There are many issues and problems that the elderly face as a result of the rapidly increasing population of elderly in the United States (as discussed in the above introduction to this chapter): parent abuse, diminishing social security benefits, discrimination, costly health care, loss of family and friends, and so on. These can be examined using sociological theories of aging and age differentiation.

Structural functional theories about aging examine aging and age differentiation in terms of the contributions that older people make to society. For example, the gradual disengagement or withdrawal of the elderly from many roles may be seen as functional for both the elderly and for society (**disengagement theory***).

Symbolic interaction theories about aging focus on how people define the aging process and the status of the aged, and on the interaction patterns of the elderly. In contrast to disengagement theory, **activity theory** says that the elderly maintain a better sense of self when they remain engaged (active) in social roles.

Exchange theories about aging examine how decreases in the power that the elderly have affects their bargaining power in a variety of situations.

Similarly, **conflict theories of aging** focus on the inequality and discrimination that the elderly face as a result of their decreasing power and resources.

Go to your introductory sociology text and study the theories of aging that it discusses.

Journal instructions:
Complete items 1 and/or 2.

1. Attend a meeting and/or interview four members of an interest group or organization for the elderly: Gray Panthers, National Retired Teachers Association, American Association of Retired Persons, National Council of Senior Citizens, or others that may be represented in your area. Ask them to identify and discuss what they think are the five most important issues that face the elderly today. Record their comments in your journal and write a paragraph about each issue that they identify.

2. Use the *Reader's Guide to Periodical Literature* to identify five different social issues or problems within the past two years that pertain specifically to the elderly. Obtain two or three newspaper or magazine articles for **each** social issue that you identified. List these, and the bibliographic information, in your journal. Read the articles and summarize in your journal what each of the five issues are concerned with. Write a paragraph for each issue.

Option: essay
Select one of the social issues or problems that you identified in your journal. Write an essay (around three to five pages, typed) in which you discuss the issue from a sociological perspective. Include the following in your discussion:

a) Use the theories of aging that apply to discuss the issue or problem. For example, how would disengagement theory explain lack of job opportunity for the elderly? What would activity theory say about this? And so on.

b) Use other relevant sociological knowledge within the chapter to discuss the issue.

Option: bibliography

Conduct library research to identify around fifteen to twenty sociological references (articles in sociology journals or books written by sociologists) that deal with the issues you identified in your journal. Your best bet is to look through the *Social Science Index*, the *Sociological Abstracts*, or any other index your library has that contains social science references. Also, look through *Gerontologist*, a journal that deals specifically with issues and problems related to the elderly. Present your references in a typed bibliography. Use the bibliographic style used in journals or in your sociology text (see Activity 1. 3).

Option: research paper

Complete the above bibliographic instructions. Then select one social issue or problem that you identified in your journal (above) for which you have at least four or five references in your bibliography and write a paper (around five to seven pages, typed) in which you explore it from a sociological point of view. What kind of focus does sociological research bring to the issue? What perspectives, theories, concepts and so on are discussed in the sociological references? What do sociologists find important and interesting about the issue or problem in question? Are there differences in the way that the issue or problem is presented, explored, and analyzed by sociologists than by journalists, news commentators, or the people you interviewed? Be sure to provide proper documentation for your references throughout your paper and include a reference page.

ACTIVITY 11. 3

Social Policy And The Elderly

As the number of social issues and problems the elderly face increases, so does the need for policies to address these issues and problems. There is debate about policies regarding mandatory retirement, pension plans, Social Security, Medicaid, Medicare, disability provisions, euthanasia, and other areas of concern for the elderly.

Research paper instructions:

1. Identify one debate or controversy regarding a policy that pertains to the elderly that has appeared in the news within the last three months. You may

need to go through back issues of newspapers and magazines to identify one. Or interview a member of an elderly interest group (see journal instructions in Activity 11. 2) for some suggestions.

2. Conduct library research to find five or six articles (either from sociology journals, news magazines, commentary magazines, congressional hearings, and so on) that present arguments for and against the policy. Be sure to collect enough articles to provide you with enough information to present a balanced discussion of the pros and cons for the policy.

3. After you conduct your library research, summarize the arguments for and against the policy in question.

4, Interview five to ten elderly people and ask them what their views are about the particular policy in question. Do they support it or oppose it? Why?

5. Write a paper (around five to seven pages, typed) in which you:
   a) Summarize what the policy (or proposed policy) is intended to accomplish and how.
   b) Present a balanced discussion of the arguments for and against the policy you identified. Base these arguments on your library research and illustrate the arguments with comments made by the people that you interviewed.
   c) Use theories of aging and age differentiation discussed in your introductory text, your library research , and your interviews to take a position for or against the policy.

Be sure to document all of your references and include a reference (works cited) page.

ACTIVITY 11. 4

How Will The Increasing Numbers Of Elderly Affect Different Occupations?

The increasing number of elderly will affect how people perform their jobs and the opportunities for employment in various professions and occupations. Identifying these occupations and examining them with sociological knowledge about the elderly could be very useful.

Instructions:
1. Carefully read the chapter on age in your introductory text. After each section you read, think of two or three occupations in which the sociological knowledge you just read about might be useful and how. They are

innumerable. Any occupation that deals with people and their needs (which is just about every occupation—medicine, law enforcement, construction, architecture, journalism, counseling, teaching, clergy, and so on) must consider the needs of the elderly, and increasingly this will be the case.

2. Interview someone from five of the occupations you identified. Discuss with them some of the ways you think that sociological knowledge of aging would be useful in their occupation. (Provide them with specific examples of sociological knowledge about the elderly that they can think about.) Ask them what types of problems and issues they face in their work in which they must consider the needs of the elderly. Write about the results of these interviews in your journal.

Option: class presentation
Complete the above journal instructions. Make a five- to ten-minute presentation to your class in which you discuss how sociological knowledge about aging is useful in particular occupations.

ACTIVITY 11. 5

How Are The Elderly Treated In Various Cultures?

Journal instructions:
Identify some people at your college or in your community from five cultures that are very different than yours. Select one from each country or culture whom you can interview or with whom you can discuss the role of the elderly in their culture. Try to have a representation of people that are from cultures that you think are very different from each other. Conduct an interview with each person and record their comments in your journal. Discuss the following with them:
   a) What is the role of the elderly in families? (For example: Are they taken into consideration when major family decisions are made? How much power do they have in the family's decisions? How important is their opinion? What is the grandparents' role with regard to grandchildren? Are the elderly treated with respect? And so on.)
   b) How are the elderly portrayed in the media: on television, movies, and so on?
   c) To what extent is ageism a problem (that is, prejudice and discrimination toward the elderly)?
   d) How is the aging process perceived in their culture? (For example, is getting older valued or de-valued?)
   e) Are the elderly treated with equality?

e) In general, what do they see as the differences between how the elderly are treated in the United States with how they are treated in the culture in which they are from?

Option: research paper
Select one culture from which you interviewed a person for your journal. Be sure that the culture is different than your own. Conduct library research about sociological issues related to the elderly in the culture that you selected. Locate three or four sociological articles and/or books about the role of the elderly, age stratification, government policies related to the elderly, social problems of the elderly, social characteristics of the elderly, and so on for the culture that you selected. Identify similar types of articles or books about the elderly in your own culture.   Use your library research and any relevant information from your journal interview to write a paper (around five pages, typed) in which you compare aging and age differentiation between your own culture and the culture you selected.   Be sure to provide proper documentation throughout your paper and include a reference (works cited) page.

CHAPTER 12

Family Groups and Systems

Politicians, journalists, and others often suggest that a decline in family values is the cause of numerous social problems - teenage pregnancy, poverty, racial conflict, divorce, drug use, unemployment, educational underachievement, and so on. Sociologist Arlene Skolnick (1991) contends, though, that people engage in false nostalgia when they lament the decline of the American family and posit it as a cause of society's ills. In doing so, they invoke a false image in which families are portrayed as a single type rather than a collection of diverse social arrangements with crises of their own (Gerstel, 1992).

Certainly, the contemporary family has its share of troubles. However, these are not necessarily the result of moral failure or a decline in values. Some of these problems are the result of long-term changes that have accompanied institutional and cultural changes. For example, divorce rates have been increasing (except for a brief period during the 1950s) and sexual norms have been changing steadily since the middle of the nineteenth century. According to sociological research (for example, Skolnick, 1991), these changes are the result not of immorality or declining values, but of changes in the economy, demography, and culture of the United States. Nor do the problems that families face indicate that families are in a state of decline. The divorce rate remains high, but so does the rate of remarriage. Most Americans (even more than a decade ago) still value the intimacy and commitment that a family provides. As Gerstel (1992, p. 442) states in her review of Skolnick's *Embattled Paradise: The American Family in an Age of Uncertainty:* "Marriage is in, not only among white and affluent black heterosexuals, but also among lesbians and gays. Parenthood is in, not only in suburbia but also among black unmarried teenagers and middle-aged feminists. Yet family relations have become vulnerable to new types of conflict and strain."

According to sociologists, the family is changing as a result of social forces, not because of moral failure or lack of values.

ACTIVITY 12. 1

What Is Family?

Traditionally, a family has been defined as "a group of kins united by blood, marriage, or adoption, who share a common residence for some part of their lives, and who assume reciprocal rights and obligations with regard to one another" (Eshleman, et al, 1993, p. 309). Today, however, the definition of the family is not so narrow. There are families without children, dual career families, blended families, single parent families, same sex marriages, unmarried cohabiting couples, and many other types of family structures.

Journal instructions:
1. Identify and read about the different family forms that are discussed in your introductory sociology textbook. Write a brief summary of each of these in your journal.

2. What type of family form best characterizes your current family?

3. Select three other family forms other than the type within which you live. Identify someone (friend, relative, neighbor, and so on) from each of the three types that you selected. Interview each of them (recording the results in your journal) to find out more about the way they live and act as a family, the types of problems they face, and so on. Here are some questions to guide your interview:
   a) Describe the family that you live with (when you are not living at school).
   b) Why do you consider yourselves a family? That is, what characteristics do you have as a group that make you a family?
   c) Describe the role relationships between family members (for example, the division of labor for family duties, the stratification system in the family, who makes the rules, and so on).
   d) What are a few of the major problems and issues that your family faces in everyday life?

4. If possible, spend at least one hour with each of the families from which you interviewed someone, or with families similar to theirs. Observe their everyday routines, activities, problems, issues, interactions, and so forth and record these observations in your journal.

5. Compare the four families that you observed (yours and the three others). What are the similarities and differences in their structure, role relationships, problems, issues, values, and so on? Based upon this journal exercise, develop a definition of family that encompasses all the types that you observed.

Option: essay
Use the information you collected in your journal to write an essay (around three to five pages, typed) in which you answer the question, "What is family?"

Option: research paper
Conduct library research to obtain three or four articles from sociology journals and/or books about one of the above types of families that you explored (other than your own). Write a paper (around five pages, typed) in which you discuss the structure, role relationships, problems, issues, or other aspects of the family about which you conducted your library research. Use proper documentation throughout your paper and include a reference page.

ACTIVITY 12. 2

Who Is Your Family?

Most of us have two families: a family of orientation and a family of procreation. A **family of orientation** is the nuclear family into which you were born and/or reared. A **family of procreation** is the family that you create when you form your own family. This often makes our lives complicated since we have roles to fulfill in each of our families. Conflict sometimes occurs between spouses because of role conflict and role strain that stem from their families of orientation and procreation. (If you need to refresh your memory about role conflict and role strain, reread the appropriate sections in you introductory text.)

Journal instructions:
1. In your journal, make an outline or a diagram of the following:
   a) your family of orientation. (Note that **your** family of orientation is probably your parents' family of procreation.)
   b) the family of orientation for each of your parents;
   c) the family of procreation for yourself and/or any of your siblings if any of you are married or have started your own families.
   d) the family of orientation for your or each of your siblings' spouses.

2. In your journal, identify and discuss problems that exist within your family that are due to role conflicts and role strains resulting from the overlap of families of orientation and procreation.

3. Is it possible to make a clear-cut distinction between families of orientation and families of procreation? Do different ones take precedence in your decision making at different times? When? Explain your answers in your journal.

Option: essay
Write an essay (around three to five pages, typed) in which you discuss the ways (as described in your journal) in which the overlap between families of orientation and procreation can create problems within families. How might such problems be resolved?

ACTIVITY 12. 3

Using Theoretical Perspectives To Examine Families

The major theoretical perspectives of sociology - structural functionalism, conflict theory, symbolic interactionism, exchange theory, and others - can be used to examine the family. Review these theories in your text as they are discussed in the chapter on family and the chapter on social theory.

Journal instructions
1. In your journal, write a summary of what the focus of each of the above theories would be in examining families.

2. For structural functionalism, conflict theory, symbolic interactionism and at least one other theoretical perspective, develop a list of questions that each perspective would lead you to ask or explore about families. For example, for structural functionalism you might ask: How do families provide the major functions of socialization, affection, emotional support, sexual regulation, reproduction, and social placement? How are role relationships interrelated in families? How are the functions of roles among family members interdependent? And so on. For conflict theory, you might ask: How are conflicts within families the result of power struggles between family members? What are the scarce resources that the struggle is about? And so on.

3. Examine your own family using the questions you developed for each of the theoretical perspectives. For each of the different perspectives that you developed questions, spend about two hours observing and thinking about relationships within your own family.

4. Discuss in your journal how these theoretical perspectives might be useful in helping a marriage counselor or someone else who works with families (for example, a clergy-person, divorce mediator, and others).

Option: essay
Write an essay (around five pages, typed) in which you discuss your family from the point of view of each of the perspectives from which you observed it and described it in your journal.

ACTIVITY 12. 4

Social Policies And The Family

Social policies concerning abortion, child care, taxes, maternity and paternity leave, sexual practices, homosexual marriages, child custody, and many others are repeatedly the subject of much political debate.

Journal instructions:
1. Look through issues of local newspapers and a major national newspaper (such as *The New York Times, Los Angeles Times, Washington Post,* and so on) for the past two months. Identify all the social policy controversies or debates that have been discussed in the news that would affect families.

2. In your journal, summarize what each of the policy debates is about. Be sure to keep a record of the newspapers, dates, page numbers, and so on that you used for your information.

3. For each policy debate that you identified, briefly explain how the policy would affect families.

Option: bibliography
1. Select one of the policy debates that you identified above in order to conduct further research about it.

2. Using your library's indexes (see Activity 3. 1) develop a bibliography of ten to fifteen articles in the popular literature (newspapers, news magazines, commentary magazines, and so on) and in the social science literature that address the policy debate that you identified. Find articles that can provide you with information about various positions on the policy debate and articles that can provide you with sociological research that can provide some insights into the debate. Be sure you have a good balance between journal articles and popular articles. Type your bibliography using the bibliographic style found in the sociology journals (see Activity 1. 3).

Option: research paper
Complete the above journal and bibliographic instructions. Write a paper (around five to seven pages, typed) in which you:
  a) Introduce the policy debate and discuss what the various positions are.
  b) Discuss at least three reasons to support the policy. Be sure to provide quotes, excerpts, or other references.
  c) Discuss at least three reasons to oppose the policy. Again, provide quotes, excerpts, or other references.
  d) Use ideas contained within your introductory text's chapter on the state of American families today to take a position for or against the policy.

Provide proper documentation of your references throughout the paper and include a reference page.

ACTIVITY 12. 5

Using Census Data To Examine The Family

Much social science research about the family uses data that is available in the national, state, and local census.

Journal instructions:
1. Locate a copy of the most recent national, state, and local census in your library.

2. Examine each census and make a list in your journal of all of the types of data that are available about families. The list is extensive and contains things such as head of household, number of children, income, divorce rates, and so on.

3. Select five types of data that you think indicate the state of the American family (for example, divorce rate, number of children, and so on). Use these five items to compare families in the nation, your state, and your city in 1990 and in 1980. For example, what was the divorce rate in the nation, your state, and your city in 1990 and in 1980? How many female-headed households were there in each in 1990 and in 1980? And so on.

4. Briefly summarize your findings. What were the changes? What remained the same? What do you think can account for the changes?

5. Locate three articles in current sociology journals that use census data about the family. Use the *Social Science Index* to locate articles that pertain to the types of data you found in the census, or look through issues of recent sociology journals such as *The Journal of Marriage and the Family, Family Relations,* or other journals that focus on family issues. What types of census data are used in these articles and for what purpose?

6. Identify three occupations in which the types of data that you found in the census or in the articles you located could be useful and explain how.

ACTIVITY 12. 6

A Cross-cultural Look At Families

It is important for you to understand that the characteristics of families and the ways that families are organized vary widely from culture to culture. Families do not exist in a vacuum but are affected by the sociocultural forces in which they exist. There are many structural patterns around which families are organized and these depend upon the culture. These patterns pertain to norms for choice of marriage partner, number of marriage partners, residence, descent and inheritance, and authority.

Journal instructions:
1. Reread the section on patterns of family organization in the chapter on families in your introductory text. In your journal, identify and define each of the patterns (as mentioned above) around which families may be organized and each of the possible forms that each pattern can take. For example, **norms of residence** may be **neolocal, patrilocal,** or **matrilocal**; **norms of authority** may be **patriarchal, matriarchal,** or **egalitarian**; and so forth. For further explanation of these patterns, consult a sociology of the family textbook (for example, Eshleman, 1993; Skolnick, 1992; or many others).

2. Describe the structural patterns around which <u>your</u> family of orientation is organized.

3. Briefly explain why each of the patterns that pertain to families within your culture make sense within the context of your culture. For example, why is monogamy the norm for number of spouses within your culture? Why is endogamy the norm for choice of marriage partner? And so on.

4. Identify a person you know who is from a culture where the structural patterns around which families of orientation are organized are very different than your culture's. (For example, if you are from the United States, find someone whose cultural background is Indian, Chinese, Japanese, Russian, or others.) From the person you identified, obtain information about the structural patterns around which families in his or her culture are organized. As you did with patterns of your own culture, ask the person to explain why each particular pattern makes sense within the culture that it is found. For example, why do arranged marriages make sense in the context of Indian culture? Why does egalitarianism make sense within American culture? And so on?

5. Identify three occupations in which knowledge of structural family pattens in different cultures may be helpful, and briefly discuss how.

Option: bibliography
Complete the above journal instructions. Then, through library research, compile a bibliography of ten to fifteen sociology articles and/or books (excluding textbooks) about various aspects of the structural patterns around which families in the culture you examined (not yours) are organized. You do not have to restrict yourself to only obtaining references about one structural pattern, such as norms for choice of marriage partner, or norms regarding authority. Type your bibliography following the bibliographic format found in sociology journals (see Activity 1. 3).

Option: research paper
Write a paper (around five pages, typed) in which you use your journal and three or four articles from your bibliography (or, if necessary find additional references) to compare the way families in your culture and another culture are different with regard to <u>one</u> structural pattern. For example, compare norms of mate selection in the U.S. and India; or compare norms of authority between the U.S. and Japan; or others. There are many things you can discuss in your paper. For example: Describe the particular structural pattern. How is it relevant to the culture? How did it develop? How is it enforced? Is it problematic in contemporary society? How has it changed over the last few generations? And so forth.

ACTIVITY 12. 7

Who Will Your Spouse Be?

Do you ever wonder what your spouse will be like? What will he look like? Will she be intelligent? What religion will he be? Will she have a good job? And so on. You probably know a great deal more about what your spouse will be like than you realize. This is because there are particular social and cultural factors that influence our choice of spouse. Many of us like to fantasize that our choice of marriage partner results from some type of non-rational attraction to another that we have no conscious control over. This may be the case in some instances. But usually, our choices of marriage partners are less likely to be attributed to chance and chemistry than to rational choice.

Journal instructions:
1. Reread the section on choice of marriage partners or mate selection in the chapter on family in your introductory sociology text. In your journal, briefly discuss the norms for choice of marriage partner that exist within your culture. Do you have free choice or arranged marriages, or some combination of both in your culture? Do you have norms of endogamy or exogamy regarding choice of spouse?

3.   Based upon your culture's and family's norms regarding choice of marriage partner, make a list of characteristics that you would probably not consider, would be prohibited or discouraged from considering, or would not have the opportunity to consider (because you wouldn't have the opportunity to meet such a person) for a marriage partner. Consider the following characteristics, or others that you can think of: age, gender, race, religion, ethnicity, education, political values, beliefs, social class, physical appearance, and so on.   For example, are there any ages of people that you would probably not consider, be prohibited from marrying, or would not have the opportunity to meet?   Any religions that you would not consider (or would not be allowed to consider)? And so on.

4.   Look at each of the characteristics of marriage partners that you have eliminated.   In your journal, briefly explain the social forces that led you to eliminate each of those characteristics.

5.   Now that you know who you would not like to marry, would not be allowed to marry, or would have no opportunity to marry, list the possibilities of each characteristic that you would consider, would be allowed to consider, and would have the opportunity to meet someone with that characteristic.

Option: essay
Use your sociological knowledge of mate selection and your journal reflections to write a scenario (around three pages, typed) in which you discuss where you might be likely to meet your spouse, what types of characteristics he or she is likely to have, how you come to realize that this person might be a potential spouse, how various social and cultural forces might influence the suitability of this person as a potential spouse (for example, how your parents, friends, and neighbors react), and so on. Have fun with this one. You will enjoy reading it again some time in the future.

CHAPTER 13

Religious Groups and Systems

Religion has always been an important part of every society and of the lives of human beings. Religious beliefs give meaning to life, serve as a source of personal gratification, and offer a relief from the frustrations of daily life. Religious ceremonies and rituals are a source of personal identity and social cohesion. Sociologists study how religion is organized, how it affects the members of a given society, how it affects and is affected by other social institutions and how religious beliefs change over time.

One aspect of religion that has been especially interesting to sociologists is the relationship between religion and politics. Some religious groups wield an enormous amount of political power. One of the most powerful religious forces that has been influencing the course of American politics lately is a faction of the Southern Baptist Convention known as **fundamentalists.** This is the belief that the teachings of the Bible must be taken literally. Fundamentalists widely supported the presidencies of Ronald Reagan and George Bush. Their impact has been felt on many political issues. For example, fundamentalists have lobbied to oppose abortion, the Equal Rights Amendment (ERA), and gay rights, and to favor prayer in schools, corporal punishment, and many forms of legislation that support traditional gender roles. The increasing role of fundamentalism in society and particularly in American politics—and in the politics of other countries as well—is important to sociologists because it demonstrates how religion is organized, how it gets its power, and how it affects society.

ACTIVITY 13. 1

Religion And Politics

The First Amendment of the U.S. Constitution requires the separation of church and state. Yet, as suggested in the introduction above, religious groups are increasingly exercising their influence and control over American political life.

Journal instructions:
1. Identify news items from the past year about seven different political issues or policies on which religious groups have tried to exert their influence (for example, corporal punishment, AIDS research, homosexual rights, abortion, child care, condoms in schools, school prayer, and so on). Use the *Reader's Guide to Periodical Literature, Newsbank*, or other indexes that your library has. To begin, look under "religion," "religious groups," "religion and politics," or specific issues that you think involved religious groups.

2. In your journal, record the name and source of each news item you find, and briefly summarize each article. Answer the following:
    a) Which religion or religious group is involved?
    b) What is the issue or policy that they are concerned with?
    c) What is their position on the issue or policy?
    d) Who are they trying to influence (political party, committee, and so on)?
    e) How are they exerting pressure (that is, what tactics are they using to try to obtain their goal)?
    f) How did politicians respond to the pressure from the group (agree, disagree, dismiss, and so on)?

Option: bibliography
Conduct library research to compile a bibliography of fifteen to twenty sociology articles and books that discuss the relationship between religion and political processes. (See, for example, Jelen, 1991; Ammerman, 1990; Wuthnow, 1989; Aho, 1991; Eve and Harrold, 1991; and many others.) Use the *Social Science Index, Sociological Abstracts*, and the journal *Contemporary Sociology* to locate relevant articles and books. Type your bibliography following the style used in sociology journals (see Activity 1. 3).

Option: research paper
Select four references (articles or books) from your bibliography about one religious group or one particular issue that religious groups have tried to influence. Write a five- to seven-page paper, typed, in which you discuss the political impact of the religious group you selected or discuss how a particular issue in American politics has been influenced by religious groups. Provide proper documentation throughout your paper and include a reference page.

ACTIVITY 13. 2

How Non-Religious Groups And Events Can Serve Religious Functions

As mentioned above in the introduction to this chapter, religion has always been an important part of individual and social life. This may seem contradictory with your observations that many people are not active participants in an organized religion. However, if we look closely at some non-religious groups and events in which people are involved, we can see that they may have similar characteristics and may serve many of the same functions as organized religion does.

Emile Durkheim defined religion as a unified system of beliefs and practices regarding sacred things that unites its followers into a single moral community. According to Durkheim, religion consists of something **sacred,** a set of **beliefs** about the sacred thing, **rituals** surrounding the sacred thing, and a **community of believers** (or **church**) that adhere to the beliefs and rituals. In addition, Durkheim, Weber, Marx, and other social theorists have identified various functions and dysfunctions of religion.

Journal instructions:
1.   Reread the chapter on religion in your introductory text and pay particular attention to the sections that discuss the definitions, functions, and dysfunctions of religion. Briefly summarize these in your journal.

2. Select a non-religious group of which you are a member or would like to learn more about (for example, fraternity, sorority, club, team, and so on) or an event/activity in which you partake regularly or would like to learn more about (for example, attending Grateful Dead concerts, attending sports events, and so on) that might have the characteristics of religion that Durkheim described. Be a participant observer of the group or event for two or three hours and/or interview a member of the group or someone (other than yourself) who partakes in the activity. In your journal, identify and describe:
   a) something that the group considers sacred or is a sacred part of the event/ activity;
   b) the beliefs about the sacred object;
   c) the rituals which are used to affirm the beliefs about the sacred object;
   d) the community of believers or church that share the beliefs and partake in the rituals;
   e) the religious functions and dysfunctions of the group (that is, identify and describe how the group or event serves the same types of functions and dysfunctions as religion).

Option: essay
Pretend that you are an anthropologist or sociologist and examine the group or activity as if it were a religion in a culture that you are observing. Write an essay, around three to five pages, typed, in which you describe the "religion" that you observed. Be sure to approach this from the perspective of cultural relativism. That is, avoid passing any judgments about the religion and discuss it in terms of the social and cultural context in which it exists. Have fun and be creative with this essay, but be sure to use relevant sociological definitions, concepts, theories, and so on.

ACTIVITY 13. 3

Using Sociological Theories To Examine Religion In Everyday Life

The major theoretical perspectives in sociology can be used to examine religion in social life. From the **structural functionalist** perspective, religion is examined in terms of what it does - that is, its functions - for society. From this perspective religion is generally seen as fulfilling social functions such as providing a source of social cohesion, creating a community of believers, cultivating social changes, and providing a means of social control and socialization.

From the **conflict perspective**, religion is generally viewed as a mechanism used by the dominant members of society to justify their position and to maintain a system of inequality. Karl Marx's view - which characterizes the conflict perspective - is that "religion is an opiate for the masses." It is used by the powerful to quiet, pacify, and control others.

From the **symbolic interactionist** perspective, religion - like other components of society - is constructed and legitimated through people's interactions with each other and, in turn, acts back upon the people. For example, as people worship together, sing hymns, and shout "Alleluia." they affirm the sanctity of their beliefs, thus giving their religious beliefs more power over them.

Journal instructions:
1. Review the sections in your text that discuss sociological theories of religion and briefly summarize them in your journal.

2. For one full week, keep a record in your journal of all of the situations, interactions, meetings, public and private places and so on in which some aspect of religion is invoked, portrayed, symbolized and so forth (for example, in political speeches, letters to the editor in newspapers and magazines, journalistic essays and editorials, prayer before meetings, prayer before meals, religious symbols in public and private places, and so forth).

3. Use the theoretical perspectives that you summarized above to briefly discuss each of the displays of religion that you observed. Here are some suggestions to help you:

a) From the perspective of structural functionalism you might discuss the possible manifest and latent functions and dysfunctions of the religious displays that you observed. For example, prayer before a business meeting may have provided a sense of social cohesion for the group (manifest function), may have been a good way to quiet the group down in order to start the meeting (latent function), or may have caused a sense of friction in the group between believers and non-believers (dysfunction).

b) From the perspective of conflict theory you might discuss how the religious display might have been used as a tool by dominant individuals or groups to justify their position or perpetuate inequality. For example, a politician wanting to cut programs to the poor might make reference to how God will help the truly worthy.

c) From the perspective of symbolic interactionism you might discuss how the religious display was used to reaffirm the beliefs of members of the religious community (the believers) and thus help to establish the reality and strength of a religion. For example, two or more believers may "praise the Lord" when one of them receives a raise at work, or they may "put it in the Lord's hands" when they are troubled about a decision. By their statements, they are creating a reality in which the Lord is responsible for what happens.

Option: essay
Write an essay (around four to five pages, typed) in which you use your journal observations and sociological theories to discuss the role of religion in everyday life.

ACTIVITY 13. 4

Using Census Data To Examine Correlates Of Religious Affiliation

There are a number of variables that are associated with religious affiliation: income level, educational level, race, ethnicity, and others. Do people's social classes, race, ethnicity, educational level and so on have anything to do with their religious affiliation? What percentage of lower-class people are Catholic? What percentage of African-Americans are Baptist? Are people with a college degree more likely to be Protestant? Are Jewish people more likely to be Democrats? And so on. Understanding what variables are associated with religious affiliation can be useful for people in a variety of occupations.

102

Journal instructions:
1. Go to your college library and find out what types of summary data are available in the U.S. Census and in the census in the state in which you live regarding religious affiliation. For example, are there data that indicate what percentage of people at different income levels—or education, race, ethnicity, political party, and so on—are affiliated with each religion? (Or ask your reference librarian if your library has other data that might provide information about religious affiliation.) Obtain one of these sources of data for the United States and one for your state. In your journal, make a list of the types of data about religious affiliation that are available and where they can be found.

2. In your journal, identify five occupations in which the types of data about religion you found might be useful and discuss how. For example, how would it be useful for someone who is in advertising to know that people of particular religions are likely to be in a particular social class? How would it be helpful for a minister to know that people in a particular religion are likely to have a particular educational level? How would it be helpful for a politician to know what religions people in a particular racial group are likely to be affiliated with? And so on. Give this some thought and be creative.

Option: class presentation
Make a five- to ten-minute presentation to your class in which you tell them what types of data about religious affiliation you found, where in the library they are located, and how these data might be useful in five occupations.

Option: table
Once you determine where you can find current summary data about religion and related variables, select two variables with which religious affiliation might be associated (for example, income, race, ethnicity, educational attainment, and so on). In the census (or other data sources that you used) locate the summary data that tell how each of these variables are related to religious affiliation in the U.S. and in your state. Prepare four tables that demonstrate the relationship between the variables you selected and religious affiliation: two tables (one table for each variable and religious affiliation) for U.S. data and two tables for your state's data. Be very careful in creating your tables. There are many ways tables can be set up. It is important that you understand this because the way a table is read is determined by how it is arranged. For example:

Table I - % of people in each religion by income

Income level	%Catholic	%Jewish	%Baptist etc.........	%no affiliation
below $10,999	20%	5%	etc.	
$11 - $15,999	18%	7%		
$16 - 20,000				
etc.				

The above table would read: 20% of people who make below $10,000 are Catholic. 7% of people who make $11,000 to 15,000 are Jewish. And so on.

There are many other ways to arrange a table. If you are confused or uncertain how to arrange your tables, there are a number of things you can do to help.
    a) Look in the chapter on research methods in your introductory text and/or a social science research methods text. They may have explanations on how to read tables.
    b) Look through the various tables in your introductory text in each of the chapters. Look at how they are arranged and practice reading them. There is probably an interpretation of the table nearby in the text so you can determine if you are reading it correctly.
    c) Look through some articles in sociology journals to see how tables are arranged.

Option: essay
Use material from the chapter on religion in your introductory text and the tables that you created to write an essay (around four to five pages, typed) entitled "Two Correlates of Religious Affiliation." The purpose of your essay will be to interpret the data in your tables. For example: What is the relationship between the variables you selected and religious affiliation? Why do you think this relationship exists? What are the implications of the relationship? And so forth. Use national and state data that you compiled in your tables to illustrate and discuss how these variables are (or are not) related to religious affiliation. Use the material in your text to help you discuss and interpret the tables.

Option: research paper
Complete the above journal instructions and table instructions. Then conduct library research to locate four articles from sociology journals or sociology books that discuss religious affiliation and **one** of the variables that you selected. Write a paper (around five pages, typed) in which you discuss the ways in which sociologists have explored the relationship between religious affiliation and the variable you selected. For example, if one of the variables you selected was income, locate four sociology articles that discuss religion

and income. Here are some questions or topics to consider in your discussion are:

a) What was the objective of the research each article discusses?
b) What were the conclusions of each article?
c) What are some overall conclusions that you can make about the relationship between religious affiliation and the variable in question?
d) Integrate the data from the relevant tables that you created into your discussion. Can any of the articles you found be used to help you interpret your tables? Can the information in your tables be used to illustrate the conclusions of any of the articles?

Be sure to document your references appropriately and include a reference (works cited) page.

CHAPTER 14

Educational Groups and Systems

While it is true that a high-quality education exists for some people in the United States, there is a growing need to improve the quality of education for many segments of the population. Consider the following data (*New Perspectives Quarterly,* Fall, 1990; Parillo et al., 19889; Weinberger, 1990):

• Over 23 million people in the United States (more than 13 percent of the population) are functionally illiterate (that is, they cannot fill out a job application or read a voting ballot).
• About 40 million (over 20 percent of the population) are marginally illiterate (that is, they cannot read at an eighth-grade level).
• Illiteracy is growing in the United States by about 2.3 million persons a year.
• The United States ranks forty-ninth among 158 nations in adult literacy.
• The national dropout rate for high schools is 29 percent; in inner cities, it is around 60 percent.
• Only 11 percent of Hispanic-Americans complete college by their early thirties.
• Among 11 countries surveyed by the National Science Foundation and the U.S. Department of Labor, U.S. students finished last in math and near the bottom in science.

One reason why quality of education is such a vital issue today is that the employment market in the United States requires higher educational skills than ever before. The availability of lower-level blue-collar jobs—such as in manufacturing (whether it is automobiles, office equipment, machinery, appliances, and so on)—has declined. Today's jobs increasingly require the skills needed to process information, to manage, and to provide services. The combination of decreased quality of education and an employment market that requires many advanced skills has led social scientists and policy makers to take a very close look at our educational system.

ACTIVITY 14. 1

A Cross-cultural Look At Education

It is commonplace today to hear or read about the educational achievements of students in cultures that are very different than your own. Is there a difference in the degree of intelligence or motivation between, for example, Japanese and American students? Do students in some parts of the world take their education more seriously than in other parts? Are educational systems in some cultures more effective than in others? To answer such questions with certainty would require more than anecdotes or common sense; it would require research about educational systems and the cultural values and norms regarding education in each culture in question. However, it is clear that educational systems vary—for better or for worse—throughout the world.

Journal instructions:
1. Identify a student at your college (or elsewhere) who is from a culture that is very different than yours. Discuss the following topics about education in that student's native culture and record his/her responses in your journal:
   a) Is everyone expected to go to school?
   b) At what age do children begin school?
   c) What type of school do people typically attend and at what ages (kindergarten, elementary, high school, college, and so on)? What would a typical educational path be for a well-educated person in that culture?
   d) How long is the school year?
   e) Is there a distinction between public and private school systems? Is either type perceived as being better? Who attends each?
   f) How much and what types of homework are usually assigned at the different levels of education? About how many hours per day is spent on education (attending school and doing homework)?
   g) What role does the family play in the educational process?
   i) What are some of the cultural values on education? For example, how is educational success or failure viewed and treated? Are there sanctions for success or failure? What type?

2. In your journal, discuss how your life would be different if the educational system in your culture was like that of the person you interviewed.

Option: essay
Write an essay (around five pages, typed) in which you compare education in your native culture with the culture of the person you interviewed.

Option: research paper
Conduct library research that will enable you to systematically compare education in your culture with that of the culture of the person you

interviewed. Write a paper (around five to seven pages, typed) in which you compare specific aspects of education in each culture, such as structure of school systems, cultural values of education, evaluation of students, types of skills taught, government support of education, nature of private vs. public education, and so on. Include at least four different references (articles, books, and so on) and the information from your journal (above). Provide proper documentation of your references and include a reference page.

ACTIVITY 14. 2

Using Theoretical Perspectives To Examine Educational Systems

Education can be viewed in a variety of ways. It may be viewed as helping to fulfill the needs of students and societies or it it may be viewed as helping to fulfill the needs of the dominant groups in society. Structural functional theory and conflict theory are often used to examine the various outcomes of educational systems.

Journal instructions:
1. Reread the sections that discuss structural functionalism and conflict theory in the chapter on education in your textbook. In your journal, briefly outline how each of these theoretical perspectives explain and describe educational systems. What does structural functionalism see as the manifest and latent functions of education? How does conflict theory explain education as a source of inequality and as a means of perpetuating the values of the dominant groups in society?

2. Derive a list of questions from the structural functionalist and conflict theories of education that you can use to examine your own educational experiences. For example: How were specific manifest functions of the educational system (for example, teaching the values of the larger society) taught at different grades? What were some specific latent functions (such as prolonged adolescence) that were met in educational systems you experienced? What values and norms that justified inequality were taught through a hidden curriculum? How was inequality fostered through education? And many others. Carefully construct around seven to ten questions. You will use them to reflect on your own education.

3. Reflect on your own education from elementary school through the present. Use the questions you developed to help you do this. In your journal, briefly discuss experiences that you can remember that fit the various explanations of structural functionalism and conflict theory as you outlined above. Write about as many experiences and examples as you can remember.

Option: essay
1. Spend about two to three hours observing in an elementary school in your area and about two to three hours observing in a high school. Use your time observing to try to answer as many questions that you developed above as you can. Record your observations in your journal.

2. Use your reflections (from your journal) on your own education and your observations of the schools to write an essay (around five pages, typed) in which you use structural functionalism and conflict theory to discuss education. Integrate your reflections and observations into your discussion.

ACTIVITY 14. 3

**To What Extent Does And Should a College Curriculum
Reflect Multiculturalism?**

Within recent years there has been much debate among many educators, sociologists, politicians, and members of minority groups about whether the college curriculum should reflect a variety of cultural traditions (including those specifically related to women, African-Americans, homosexuals, and other minority groups), or continue to be rooted in the Western intellectual traditions that tend to reflect white, male, Eurocentric values. The debate has become heated at times, but it seems that education at all levels is beginning to reflect multicultural traditions and values.

Journal instructions:
1. For one week, make observations at your college that can help you assess the extent to which multiculturalism is part of the curriculum and life of the school. Here are some things to look for and discuss in your journal. To what extent does each of the following reflect the views, accomplishments, and values of various cultures and groups or of white, European traditions, values and accomplishments:
   a) the titles of courses in each department (found in the college catalogue);
   b) the course descriptions found in the college catalogue;
   c) the books from a sample of courses in different departments;
   d) a sample of course syllabi from different departments;
   e) the racial, ethnic, and gender composition of the faculty;
   f) the articles and their positions in the student newspaper;
   g) the editorials and essays that appear in your school newspaper;
   h) the types of campus clubs and organizations;
   i) the cultural events sponsored by your college (plays, music, speakers, and so on).

2. Interview people from four minority groups present on your campus (for example, African-Americans, Hispanic Americans, Japanese Americans, homosexuals, women, and so on). Discuss with them how they feel about the extent to which their views and traditions are represented in the curriculum and the overall culture of the college.

Option: class presentation
Prepare a five- to ten-minute presentation in which you discuss your journal findings with your class.

Option: essay
Write a paper (three to five pages, typed) in which you use structural functionalist and conflict perspectives on education to discuss the types of cultural traditions and values that exist at your college and in the college curriculum.

Option: research paper
1. Conduct library research to find four or five articles and or books that will provide you with arguments for and against a college curriculum that reflects multiculturalism. There are many. Some examples are Eshleman, Cashion, and Basirico, 1993; D'Souza, 1991a; D'Souza, 1991b; Adler et al, 1990; Rothenberg, 1991; Magner, 1991; and many others. (Key words to search for in the indexes and references are "multiculturalism" and "political correctness.")

2. Using your journal observations, your library research, and sociological theories of education (structural functionalism and conflict theory), write a paper (around five pages, typed) in which you discuss reasons for and against having a curriculum at your college that reflects multiculturalism. Provide proper documentation throughout your paper and include a reference page.

ACTIVITY 14. 4

Educational Policies And Issues

Journal instructions:
1. Look through national and local newspapers for the past year (or use your library's periodical indexes) to identify national and local issues and policy debates about education (for example, vouchers, busing, magnet schools, decentralization, and so on). Find two or three news articles on each and, in your journal, briefly summarize what each issue and/or debate is about.

2. Conduct interviews with <u>at least</u> three of the following: a superintendent for your city or county school system, a principal of a high school or elementary school in your area, a college administrator (president, vice president, provost, dean, and so on), a local politician (city manager, county commissioner, city councilperson, and so on), a state politician, and a federal politician. Ask each person whom you interview to identify what they think the major issues and policy debates are regarding education today, what these issues and/or debates are about, and what their position is regarding the issue and/or policy debate. Record their responses in your journal

Option: essay
Using the information you obtained and developed in your journal, and material from the chapter on education in your introductory sociology text, write an essay (about five pages, typed) describing issues and policies in education today. What are the major issues? (Obviously you cannot talk in-depth about each one in a five-page paper, so select the ones that you think are the most significant.) Is there a difference between local and national issues? How does the material in the chapter on education in your text help you to interpret the issues from a sociological perspective?

Option: research paper
1. Conduct library research about **one** of the issues or policy debates that you find particularly interesting or important. Obtain two or three articles from sociology journals or sociology books, and two or three articles that appear in the popular press (newspaper, news magazines, commentary magazines, and so on).

2. Write a paper (five to seven pages, typed) in which you discuss the issue or policy debate. Identify and describe the issue or policy in question. Illustrate it with examples from your journal (above). If it is an issue, what are some ways of dealing with it? If it is a policy debate, what are the arguments for and against the policy? What sociological theories, concepts, or ideas can be used to help explain or provide some insight about the issue or policy in question? In your paper, be sure to integrate material from the chapter on education in your text, your library research, and your journal. Provide proper documentation throughout your paper and include a reference page.

ACTIVITY 14. 5

Education And Social Stratification

Like other social systems, schools reflect social stratification and can perpetuate further inequality. This is not necessarily the result of the curriculum itself or the quality of the teachers in the schools, but may be the result of other opportunities and life chances that are related to educational systems. This was illustrated well in two movies about two different types of education systems: *Dead Poets Society* and *Stand and Deliver*. Obtain a copy of each of these movies. They should be readily available at your local video rental store or in your college library.

Journal instructions:
1. Go to your introductory sociology text and reread the chapters (or review your notes) on education, social stratification, socialization, and minority groups.

2. View the above movies and, in your journal, answer (or discuss) the following questions about each:
   a) Describe the social characteristics of the students who attend each school (for example, social class, previous education, ethnicity, race, gender, and so on).
   b) What stereotypes and prejudices toward the students are held by teachers, administrators, parents, members of the community, and so on?
   c) Discuss the results of these stereotypes and prejudices in terms of Cooley's "looking glass self" theory and in terms of a "self-fulfilling prophecy."
   d) What is taught in each school (curriculum, types of courses, values, and so on)?
   e) What opportunities or contacts for college and jobs are available to students in each school?
   f) What happens to students in each school when they get into trouble?
   g) Use structural functional and conflict theories of education to discuss education in each of these movies.

Option: essay
Write an essay (around three to five pages, typed) in which you use sociological knowledge (theories, concepts, research findings, and so on) to review and analyze both movies.

Option: research paper
1. Conduct library research to locate four or five sociology articles from journals or books (excluding textbooks) about inequality and education.

3. Write a paper (around five to seven pages, typed) in which you apply the information you compiled in your journal, sociological knowledge from your textbook, and information from your library research to analyze the above movies. You might use the movies to illustrate sociological ideas, or you might use sociological ideas to analyze the movies, or a combination of both. Provide proper documentation throughout your paper and include a reference page.

CHAPTER 15

Political Groups and Systems

An important area of sociological research about political groups and systems concerns **interest groups**. Interest groups are organizations that attempt to influence the government to support policies that benefit particular collectivities. There are interest groups for farmers, physicians, teachers, women, automobile manufacturers, house builders, AIDS sufferers, and nearly every other occupation, industry, and group that would benefit from particular types of policies.

One way that interest groups work is through **lobbying**. Lobbying consists of writing letters, making telephone calls, sending petitions to members of Congress, organizing rallies, meeting with politicians, and so on to try to persuade legislators to vote for or against a particular regulation or policy such as abortion rights, gun control, affirmative action, environmental regulation, AIDS research, and many others.

Sometimes interest groups hire **consultants** who are particularly knowledgeable about how to influence or have special contacts with government legislators. Often, consultants for interest groups are former members of Congress or the Cabinet.

Interest groups may also use **public relations** experts to try to win support for a policy by shaping public opinion on an issue. Elected government officials are more likely to support a policy if they know the voters support it.

Finally, interest groups may sponsor **political action committees (PACs)**. PACs are organizations formed to raise money for political campaigns. By making contributions to the political campaigns of candidates, an interest group can help a politician they feel is sympathetic to their views get elected.

The practice of trying to influence government policies has always been a legitimate part of the American political process. However, when it is based upon political contacts rather than knowledge, and upon how much a group can afford to spend to achieve its political goals, it raises important questions

113

about the nature of political systems themselves. Do political systems reflect the common values and interests of a society, or do they reflect the values and interests of those who have the most power and wealth? Do all the people have a say in the policies that govern people, or does a ruling elite determine policy? If it is a ruling elite, who are they, and how do they maintain their power?

There are many other issues that illustrate the concerns of sociologists regarding political systems.

ACTIVITY 15. 1

Whose Interests Are Represented By Interest Groups?

Journal instructions:
1. Review the sections about interest groups and theories of political systems in your introductory sociology text.

2. Look through past issues of national and local newspapers or magazines to identify five different interest groups that have tried to influence legislation about specific issues or policies during the past six months. (Or use your library's indexes—for example, *Reader's Guide to Periodical Literature*, *Newsbank*, or others.) Record these in your journal.

3. Locate, read, and note in your journal two or three news reports (in newspapers, news magazines, commentary magazines, and so on) about each of the five interest groups and what they were trying to accomplish. Then, for each interest group you identified, use the news reports to briefly discuss the following:
   a) Identify the group or organization that the interest group represents.
   b) What did they try to accomplish?
   c) What methods did they use to influence legislators (lobbying, consulting, public relations, or anything else)? Describe how they did this.
   d) Who did they try to influence?
   e) Do you think the interest group—in their attempt to represent a particular group or organization—represents common social values (that is, values that would benefit most of society), or do you think that they represent primarily the interests of a particular group?
   f) Do you think that the type of influence used by the interest group was legitimate? Do you think that it was fair to all groups who may have had different positions on the issue or policy in question? Why or why not?
   g) How successful do you think the interest group was (or might be) in influencing government legislation?

114

Option: essay
1. Interview two local, state, or national politicians (one Republican and one Democrat) about the role of interest groups in influencing legislation. Make a list of interview questions based on the items in question three above. (For example: What are some examples of issues or policies that interest groups have tried to exert influence over? Who did they represent? How did they try to persuade you or other legislators? And so on.)

2. Based upon what you have compiled in your journal and your interviews, write an essay (around five pages, typed) in which you use structural functional and conflict theories of political systems to discuss interest groups.

Option: research paper
1. Select one of the interest groups that you identified above. Conduct further library research (five or six articles and/or books) to find out more about this group. Locate a variety of sources: articles from sociology journals, sociology books, commentaries, news, and so on. The *CQ Researcher* (called *Congressional Quarterly's Editorial Research Reports* before 1992) is an excellent source of articles that contain summaries of research and bibliographies on a wide range of social issues. Obtain information about: the history of the group, how it is organized, who its leaders are, some of the issues and policies in which they have been involved, the specific groups or organizations that they represent, the methods that they have used to exert influence, how successful they have been, their financial backing, the size of their membership, and their political ideology.

2. To help you obtain the above information, observe at least one of the following: a rally or meeting sponsored by the interest group you selected, an office out of which the interest group operates, or a PAC office sponsored by the interest group. You can probably find out about your local PACs or interest groups through you local government office or Chamber of Commerce.

3. Obtain some specific examples—petitions, media advertising, pamphlets, video tapes, and so on—of how the interest group has tried to exert influence (through lobbying, consulting, public relations, and so on).

4. Write a paper (around five to seven pages, typed) in which you use structural functional and conflict theories of political systems to discuss the interest group about which you conducted your research. Provide proper documentation throughout your paper and include a reference page.

ACTIVITY 15. 2

Uses Of Power And Authority In Everyday Life

Power is the ability to control the behavior of others. While power is most often thought about in terms of political systems, power is also used in our everyday lives: at work, in school, in personal relationships, at church, and so on. Go to your introductory text and review the types of power: **physical force, latent force,** and **legitimate power** (**traditional authority, charismatic authority, and rational-legal authority**.

Journal instructions:
1. Identify items that have appeared in the news within the last few months that illustrate each of the above types of power and authority. In your journal, write a brief summary of each news item, where it is from (newspaper or magazine, date, and page), the type of power it illustrates, and how.

2. For one week, keep a record in your journal of your observations of how power and authority are used in everyday life (the power and authority that you are subject to, that you use, and that you observe others using in various situations). Here are a few examples of situations to observe (do not feel limited to these only):
   a) a political campaign speech, address, or press conference;
   b) the way that family members (parents, children, spouses, and so on) attempt to control each other;
   c) how teachers, administrators, and students attempt to control each other;
   d) the way in which people try to control others in their work (other employees or clientele);
   e) the way in which religious leaders try to control their congregation;
   f) how people in intimate relationships attempt to control one another.

3. For each of your observations that you record in your journal:
   a) Briefly describe each situation and discuss the type of power or authority that was used. What was the source of the power?
   b) In your view, was the type of power used an appropriate way to obtain the goal of the person or group exercising the power?
   c) Did the type of power used achieve the intended goal of the person or group exercising the power?

4. Identify five occupations in which you might be interested. Think about the types of situations that require power in these occupations and briefly discuss what types of power would be most effective.

Option: essay
Based upon your above journal work, write a paper (around four to five pages, typed) in which you discuss the types of power that tend to be used in various types of situations and the types of power that are most effective in various situations.

ACTIVITY 15. 3

Political Socialization

Political socialization refers to the ways in which people are encouraged to adopt particular political perspectives, attitudes, values, and beliefs. Political socialization occurs in much the same way as any other socialization, beginning at a very young age and continuing throughout the life cycle. Go to your introductory sociology text and reread the chapter on socialization.

Journal instructions:
1. In your journal, briefly describe your current political views and affiliation. Include descriptions of such things as overall political philosophy (conservative, liberal, middle of the road, or anything else), party preference, degree of political activism (for example, are you a member of any political clubs such as the Young Democrats, how often do you participate in political rallies or attend demonstrations, do you write to your congressperson about issues that concern you, do you vote regularly, do you campaign for candidates, and so on), political views on particular issues (abortion, gun control, taxes and so on), and anything else that describes your political views and affiliation.

2. After you have completed the description of your political self, think about the ways in which you have come to have these particular perspectives and behaviors. Think about and discuss in your journal the ways you have been socialized through various agents of socialization during your childhood and adolescence. For example:
   a) Did members of your family have any particular political preferences? Were they politically active? Were they involved in any occupation that tended to favor particular political attitudes?
   b) Were you politically socialized in school in any way? Did you begin each day with the Pledge of Allegiance? How politically active were the parents of the students who attended the school and what were their views?
   c) Did you receive any form of political socialization from your religious affiliations? Did religious leaders make their political views explicitly known and encourage the congregation to vote in particular ways about particular issues?

d) What types of political views and behaviors did your friends have? Were they conservative, liberal, Democratic, Republican? Were they very politically active?

e) What was the overall political climate when you were growing up? Who was president? Who were your state and local politicians?

3. While much of our political perspective is shaped through early socialization, it continues to be shaped throughout our adult life. For one week, keep a record in your journal of your observations of how political socialization occurs in your daily life. Carefully observe and consider how family, religion, peers, school, the media, reference groups, in-groups, politicians, and other agents of socialization influence your political attitudes and behaviors.

Option: class presentation
Make a five- to ten-minute presentation to your class in which you describe to them the ways in which you have been and continue to be politically socialized.

Option: essay
Write an essay (around five pages, typed) in which you present an autobiographical account of your past and present political socialization, and your predictions about your future political attitudes and behaviors.

Option: research paper
Conduct library research to find four or five articles in sociology journals or sociology books that discuss political socialization. Your best bet is to look in the *Social Science Index*, *Sociological Abstracts*, and the journal *Contemporary Sociology*. You may also want to look into some political science journals regarding the topic of political socialization. Write a paper (around five to seven pages, typed) in which you use the information contained in the articles and/or books you found to discuss your own political socialization and your observations of political socialization in everyday life that you wrote about in your journal. Use your library research to explain what you have observed, or use your observations as illustrations of what the articles discuss, or both. Provide proper documentation throughout your paper and include a reference page.

ACTIVITY 15. 4

Who Rules America?

There are two general views about how major decisions are made in America. The **elitist view** holds that major government decisions are made by a relatively small, close-knit group of leaders who have similar political and economic interests. The **pluralist view** contends that decisions are made through a process in which the interests of many different groups are represented. There are a variety of theories related to each of these views. Carefully read about the elitist and pluralist theories in your introductory sociology text.

Instructions:
1. Look through past issues of newspapers, news magazines, or commentary magazines in order to identify a political decision that you think illustrates (or at least appears to illustrate) elitism and one that illustrates pluralism. For example, do you think a particular Supreme Court appointment illustrates elitism or pluralism? Do you think a decision to become involved in a war illustrates elitism or pluralism? Do you think that selling arms to a foreign country illustrates elitism or pluralism? Do you think enacting a particular tax policy illustrates elitism or pluralism? And so on.

2. Conduct further library research about each of these political decisions. Use a wide variety of references that can provide you with further insights about each: articles in sociology journals, news magazines, commentary magazines, reviews of government proceedings (such as the *Congressional Digest, CQ Researcher*, and so on). Look for articles that contain information about how the decisions were made, who made them, whose political, economic, or social interests the decision benefitted, and so on. You may need to find four or five references for each decision you select in order to obtain the information you need.

3. How does the information you found support the elitist or pluralist explanations of political systems? Are there any particular elitist or pluralist theories that apply to what you have found? Write a paper (around five pages, typed) in which you use the information you obtained about the political decisions, elitist and pluralist theories, and theories about political systems (structural functionalism and conflict theory) to discuss the question, "Who rules America?" Provide proper documentation throughout your paper and include a reference page.

CHAPTER 16

Economic Groups and Systems

In 1992, during the doldrums of the American economy, many politicians and American automobile manufacturers berated the American public for not buying American products, and criticized Japan for exporting so many products to the United States. Many insisted that buying products made by American corporations, such as General Motors, would revitalize the American economy. Consider, however, the following profile—offered by Harvard economist Robert Reich—of the way in which a typical General Motors automobile is produced and how the consumer's money is distributed (Reich, 1992). When an American buys a Pontiac LeMans:
- about $3,000 goes to South Korea for routine labor and assembly operations;
- about $1,850 goes to Japan for advanced components such as engines and electronics;
- about $700 goes to western Germany for styling and design engineering;
- about $400 goes to Taiwan, Singapore, and Japan for small components;
- about $250 goes to Britain for advertising and marketing;
- about $50 goes to Ireland and Barbados for data processing;
- about $4,000 goes to strategists in Detroit, bankers and lawyers in New York, lobbyists in Washington, insurance and health-care workers all over the country and to GM shareholders—most of whom live in the United States but a growing number of whom are foreign nationals.

General Motors, like many other very large corporations such as Ford, Chrysler, Volkswagen, International Telephone and Telegraph Corporation (IT&T), Beatrice, General Electric, Pepsico, CocaCola, Shell, Exxon, and many others, is a **multinational corporation**. A multinational corporation owns companies in one or more foreign nations where they employ workers and produce and sell their products. For better or for worse, the existence of multinational corporations has an enormous impact on the state of the American economy and American peoples' lives.

120

ACTIVITY 16. 1

Multinational Corporations

Read the sections about multinational corporations in your introductory sociology textbook.

Journal instructions:
1. Identify three multinational corporations that you would like to learn about. Select from those mentioned in the introduction above or consult with an economics or business professor at your school for some other suggestions. Select corporations that manufacture different products or provide different services. (That is, if you select GM, do not select Ford, Chrysler, or Volkswagen.)

2. Find ten to twenty articles about these multinational corporations that have appeared during the past year or two in financial newspapers and magazines (such as *The New York Times, The Wall Street Journal, Forbes, Business Week),* and others (your library's indexes should be very useful here) that will enable you to answer the following questions:
   a) What types of national and international issues and policies (such as trade agreements, tariffs, foreign policy, and many others) affect the policies, operation, or success of the corporation? List and discuss each of these in your journal using information from the articles that you found.
   b) What types of issues and policies (related to areas such as family, health care, employment, income, environment, and many others) that affect people in the U.S. and other countries does the corporation's policies create? List and discuss each of these in your journal using information from the articles that you found.

Option: class presentation
Prepare a five- to ten-minute presentation to your class in which you discuss the issues and policies that both affect and are affected by the multinational corporations you selected. Provide explicit examples from the news.

Option: essay
Read the section in your introductory sociology textbook about structural functional and conflict theories of economic systems. If your book does not discuss these in the chapter on economics, reread the section about these theories in the chapter on sociological theory and in the chapter on politics. Write an essay (around five pages, typed) in which you use the material you collected in your journal (above) to discuss multinational corporations from the point of view of structural functional theory and conflict theory.

ACTIVITY 16. 2

Taking A Cross-cultural Look At Economic Systems

An **economic system** is the social system that provides for the production, distribution, and consumption of goods and services in a society such as food, shelter, clothing, health care, education, entertainment, and many others. Like political systems, there are different types of economic systems in different societies. These systems are either some form of **capitalism**—an economic system based upon private ownership of the means of production (that is, factories, corporations, land, raw materials, equipment, money, and so on)—or **socialism**—an economic system based upon government ownership of the means of production—or a **mixed economy** such as **welfare capitalism** or **democratic socialism**. While it is easy for us to take an ethnocentric view and say that our economic system is the best - and it may be for our society - it is important to take a culturally relativist approach to examining economic systems. Is capitalism the best form of economy for all societies? Are there some societies that might benefit more from socialism or a mixed economy? How does a society's economic system affect other institutions in that society?

Journal instructions:
1. Read about the different types of economic systems described in your introduction to sociology text. Identify someone that you know that is from a country that has an economic system that is somewhat different than the capitalist system in the United States—for example, a student, a professor, or an administrator at your college, a friend or a neighbor. (If you are a student from a country other than the United States, identify someone from a country that has an economic system different than the one in your country.)

2. Have an in-depth conversation with that person about what it is like to live under an economic system different than the United States (or your country's). Discuss the following items with that person and keep notes in your journal:

    a) The economic system. What type of economic system exists in the country of the person you are interviewing - capitalist, socialist, or a mixed economy?

    b) Employment. What are the rates of unemployment in that country? Do people have the option of seeking any type of employment they wish? How difficult is it to become employed? What types of jobs are available? What are wages like for different occupations? Do most people you know tend to be satisfied with their jobs?

    c) Health care. How is the health care system different than in the U.S.? Is health care guaranteed to everyone? What is the quality of health care? Does everyone receive the same quality of health care?

d) Family policies. What type of non-parental child care exists? What types of family policies exist (maternity, family leave, and so on)?
e) Education. Is there both private and public education? Is there a difference in the quality of each?
f) Consumerism. Is there a wide variety of products—food, clothing, automobiles, and so on—available for purchase? Is the cost of products higher or lower than in your own country? Is there a difference in the quality of products from your country?
g) Housing. Is there a problem with homelessness? Are housing costs controlled? How difficult is it to find a satisfactory place to live? What are housing accommodations like?
h) Issues and problems. What are some of the most important economic issues and problems in that country? Would the country benefit from having a different type of economic system?

Option: essay
Write an essay (around three to five pages, typed) in which you discuss the functions and dysfunctions of an economic system based upon socialism (state ownership of the means of production) and the functions and dysfunctions of a system based upon capitalism (private ownership of the means of production). Use examples from your journal to illustrate your discussion.

Option: research paper
1. Conduct library research to find four or five articles from sociology journals or sociology books that address one or more of the economic issues that you identified in the country that you conducted your journal interview about. For example, you might find journal articles about how health care or education exists in a country with welfare capitalism such as Sweden or Great Britain.

2. Write a paper (around five pages, typed) in which you compare lifestyles in your country with the country about which you conducted your journal and library research. Use examples from your journal to illustrate the ideas in your paper. Provide proper documentation throughout your paper and include a reference page.

ACTIVITY 16. 3

Examining The Relationship Between The Economy And Other Social Institutions

The economic system of a society influences aspects of that society: family, health care, education, leisure time, gender roles, politics, and many others.

Journal instructions:
1. Watch a financial news television program (such as CNN Moneyline, The Nightly Business Report, or others) and read (or at least carefully look through) *The Wall Street Journal* every day for one week. In your journal, keep a record of all of the social issues that are mentioned and discussed and how they are related to economic issues.

2. After one week, summarize the types of issues that you found and briefly discuss in your journal the relationship between the economy and other aspects of society.

ACTIVITY 16. 4

Labor Unions

Labor unions have existed as a means of workers trying to improve their working conditions for centuries in countries throughout the world. Yet, they are still met with resistance in many businesses in many parts of the United States. It is important to understand the types of issues that labor unions deal with and to consider the advantages and disadvantages of labor unions for employees, businesses, and society.

Journal instructions:
1. Identify a person that you know that is a member of a labor union. Discuss with him or her—and keep a record in your journal—the types of issues that the union deals with, how helpful the union is in his/her job, and the advantages and disadvantages of having a labor union.

2. Ask your friend to take you to a local meeting of the labor union. Observe, and record in your journal, the types of issues that the union discusses, how the meeting is organized, how problems are resolved, and so forth.

3. Interview an administrator or manager at a company that has a labor union and one at a company that does not allow labor unions. Ask the administrator or manager what the advantages and disadvantages of labor unions are and why there is or is not a union present to represent the employees at that company.

4. Identify two occupations in which you think that labor unions would serve positive functions for both management and employees, and two occupations in which you think that labor unions would not be beneficial. Discuss your reasons for your choices in your journal.

124

Option: research paper
1. Conduct library research to identify a major labor dispute that has occurred within the last five years that involved a labor union. (Use your library's indexes —*Reader's Guide to Periodical Literature, Social Science Index, Newsbank,* and others —to help you do this.) Find five to ten articles from a variety of sources (newsmagazines, commentary magazines, sociology journals, and so on) that provide information about the dispute.

2. What was the dispute about? What were the pros and cons of the positions taken by the union and the pros and cons of the positions taken by those with whom they were employed (or whomever the dispute was with)? What was the outcome of the dispute?

3. Write a paper (around five pages, typed) in which you use structural functional theory, conflict theory, and other relevant theories of economic systems to discuss the labor dispute you identified and researched. Be sure to provide proper documentation of your references throughout your paper and include a reference page.

ACTIVITY 16. 5

The Changing Nature Of Work

The nature of work and the types of jobs available are changing rapidly in American society and in most other developed nations. Changes in technology (for example, the uses of computers and robots in the workplace), demography (such as the aging of society), the family (for example, the increase of dual income families), economic policies (such as minimum wage), industry (such as the growth of multinational corporations), and many other social changes have affected the types of employment that is available.

Journal instructions:
1. Compare the types of jobs that are listed in the classified section of a national newspaper and a local newspaper for one day currently and on one day on or around the same date ten years ago. List the types of jobs that are available and how many of each. Classify these jobs in terms of primary, secondary, and tertiary Note your observations in your journal. How have the types and numbers of jobs that are available changed during the last ten years?

2. Interview the employment placement counselor at your college and a placement officer that works in an employment agency. Ask them how the employment market as changed during the last ten years and note these in your journal. For example:

a) What types of skills are necessary to compete in today's job market?
b) How has the overall availability of employment changed?
c) Is there a difference in the types of jobs that are available today than were available ten years ago?
d) Taking inflation into consideration, are wages higher or lower today than ten years ago?
e) How will the changing job market affect your chances for employment and the types of jobs that you must prepare yourself for?

Option: class presentation
Prepare a presentation to your class in which you discuss how the job market has changed during the last ten years. Also, discuss with your class the employment prospects for your graduating class and the skills that will be necessary for you to successfully obtain a job.

ACTIVITY 16. 6

Let's Go To The Movies

There were a number of movies made during the 1980s and early 90s that deal with important economic issues. The functions and dysfunctions of capitalism were explored in such movies as *Norma Rae, Roger and Me, Wall Street*, and *Other People's Money*. While these are not sociological studies of economic systems, they do offer some valuable insights.

Journal instructions:
The above movies are readily available in most video stores, or perhaps at your local or college library. View three of these movies. As you view each, keep a list in your journal of all of the themes and ideas that they could be used to illustrate in your introduction to sociology textbook's chapter on economic groups and systems. After you have watched each movie, briefly discuss how each of the ideas that you identified is illustrated by the movie.

Option: essay
Pretend that you are a movie critic. Write a two-page review of each of the movies you viewed basing your critique on how the movies illustrate important sociological themes about economic systems.

CHAPTER 17

Health-Care Groups and Systems

Health care has reached center stage among important social issues in the United States and throughout the world. One particularly important issue that affects almost all Americans is the rising cost of health care.

As of the early 1990s, Americans have been spending over $730 billion a year on health care—nearly $3,000 per person. This is an increase of 193 percent since 1980. Health-care costs are projected to rise to $1.06 trillion a year by 2000 and to over $5.5 trillion by 2010. Americans spend more on health care than people in any other country. Yet, recent Census Bureau statistics indicate that over 63 million Americans - almost 30 percent of the population —are not covered by any form of health insurance or government programs such as Medicare or Medicaid. And many people who are insured have inadequate coverage (United Way of America, 1992).

There are many reasons why health-care costs continue to skyrocket, such as advances in technology which require new and expensive equipment, increasing costs of drugs, high rates of malpractice insurance for physicians, and the spread of diseases that are very expensive to treat such as the AIDS epidemic. The rising cost of health care is an important issue because it raises important questions about whether or not current systems of health care will be able to meet society's needs.

ACTIVITY 17. 1

Who Will Pay?

As indicated in the introduction above, the high cost of health care in the United States is a significant social issue. One reason this is an important issue is that the high cost determines the extent to which all members of society can receive adequate health care. Second, the high cost of health care will affect the way that other social institutions function and how they meet social needs. Third, solving the high cost issue may have implications for the way in which our entire health-care system operates, thus affecting the medical profession, other health care organizations and businesses, and the economy.

These are complex problems without easy solutions. A first step, though, is to understand what the implications of high health-care costs are, how they may affect society, and how various alternatives to the way that our current health-care system operates will affect society.

Journal instructions:
1. Discuss with your parents, spouse, or other family members the percentage of your family's annual income that goes toward health-care insurance. (If your family does not have health care insurance, what percentage of its annual income is generally spent on health care?) Think about and discuss in your journal how your family will adjust to increasing health-care costs.

2. Health-care reform is a major political, as well as social issue. Many policies have been suggested by politicians from both parties regarding how health care will be paid for and the organization of the health care system itself. Look through current and past issues of newspapers, magazines, and journals (use your library's indexes to help you locate appropriate articles) to identify <u>at least two</u> policies that have been proposed to deal with the cost of health care in the United States during recent years. In your journal, briefly outline what each of these policies proposes.

3. For each policy, think about and discuss in your journal what the implications are for your family, for the medical profession, and for health care if it were adopted.

4. Interview two physicians and two federal, state, or local politicians (one Republican and one Democrat) about the high cost of health care. Ask them what they think about the policies that you discussed in your journal (above). Also, ask each of them what they think could be done to deal with the high cost of health care in the United States.

Option: essay
1. Look through the chapter on health care in your introductory sociology text. Identify the theories, concepts, or research findings that could help you evaluate the policies you identified.

2. Write an essay (around five pages, typed) in which you discuss the policies you identified in your journal by using relevant sociological knowledge and the results of the interviews you conducted.

Option: research paper
1. Conduct library research to identify arguments for and against the enactment of two of the health care policies you identified in your journal. Use a variety of references: newspapers, magazines, commentary magazines, reviews of congressional hearings, sociology journals, and so on.

2. Write an essay (around five to seven pages, typed) in which you use your library research and interviews to:
    a) Present each policy.
    b) Present the arguments for and against each policy, including a discussion of the implications for society and the health care system.
    c) Take and support a position about one or both of these policies. For example, should both be considered? Should both be tossed out as dysfunctional for society or the health care system? Is one better than the other?

Provide proper documentation throughout your paper and include a reference page.

ACTIVITY 17. 2

Current Health-Care Issues

In your introductory sociology text, read about the different types of health care that are available in the United States today and about the perspectives on health care offered by sociological theories (structural functionalism, conflict theory, and symbolic interactionism).

Journal instructions:
1. Interview a hospital administrator, a physician, a nurse, an administrator of a Health Maintenance Organization (HMO), an insurance agent, and a chiropractor. In your journal, record their responses to the following questions:
    a) What are the two or three biggest issues or problems in health care in the United States today?
    b) What should be done to help resolve these issues or problems?
    c) Should the government play a role in resolving these issues or problems? If yes, what? If no, why not?

2. Use structural functional theory, conflict theory, and symbolic interactionism to think, and make brief comments in your journal, about the comments made by each of the people you interviewed.

ACTIVITY 17.3

AIDS-Related Social Issues

AIDS is spreading at rates which continuously outstrip previous projections. At the time of this writing over 250,000 Americans have been diagnosed with AIDS, over 1.5 million carry the human immunodeficiency virus (HIV) that precedes AIDS. The World Health Organization (WHO) estimates the total cases of AIDS worldwide at 1.5 million, with 8 to 10 million people infected with HIV. Projections of the total number of people worldwide infected with HIV by 2000 range from 30 to 110 million. The rapid spread of AIDS has led to a number of important related social issues. For example: Should condoms be distributed upon request in schools? Should there be sex education in schools? If so, at what age (or grade) should sex education begin? Should "safe sex" be a part of sex education programs? Should health-care practitioners (physicians, nurses, chiropractors, dentists, and so on) who have AIDS be allowed to continue to practice? Should health-care practitioners be required to treat AIDS sufferers? There are many others.

Journal instructions:
1. Identify as many AIDS-related issues as you can that have occurred in the news over the past five years. You do not have to go through every newspaper and magazine to do this. Rather, you can probably do this effectively by looking through a sample of months in the various periodical and news indexes in your college library (for example, *Reader's Guide to Periodical Literature, Social Science Index, New York Times Index, Newsbank,* and so on). Try to obtain fifteen to twenty articles that discuss a variety of the above issues or other issues related to AIDS.

2. In your journal, make a list of the issues for which you found articles, and list all the articles (authors, dates, publication) that pertain to each issue. Use the articles to briefly summarize what each of the issues is about.

3. Use these issues to think about and discuss in your journal what the social consequences of AIDS may be. For example, what impact might early childhood sex education have on the types of relationships that people form at different stages in their life? Try not to take a position for or against a policy or an issue. Rather, try to think of all the possible consequences— positive and negative—that each issue raises.

4. In your introductory sociology text, read about **social epidemiology**, and the different ways in which health and illness are viewed (**the social model of illness** and **the medical model of illness**). Think about and discuss in your journal how AIDS and its related issues have led to changes in which health and illness are viewed.

Option: class presentation
Make a five- to ten-minute presentation to your class in which you discuss the issues you identified and the possible short- and long-term consequences—positive and negative—for society.

Option: research paper
Conduct library research to find four or five articles in sociology journals and/or books written by sociologists that discuss the social consequences of AIDS. Write a paper (around five pages, typed) in which you present an overview of the social consequences of AIDS from the point of view of sociologists and use the issues you identified above (in your journal) to illustrate what these consequences might be. Provide proper documentation throughout your paper and include a reference page.

ACTIVITY 17. 4

A Cross-Cultural Look At Health-Care Systems

The United States is one of the wealthiest countries in the world, yet more than 30 percent of its population does not get the health care they need. Thus, it may be useful to examine health-care systems in other countries.

Journal instructions:
Interview an international exchange student or visiting professor on your campus, or someone you know, who is from a country in which government plays a greater role in health-care than in the United States (for example, Canada, Great Britain, China, Japan, or Sweden). Discuss with the student the way in which the health care system in his or her country works. Keep notes about your discussion in your journal. Here are some questions to help you get started:
 a) How expensive is health care?
 b) Do people have to pay for health care insurance?
 c) To what extent is health care operated by private health-care practitioners and by the government?
 d) In general, how is the quality of health care?
 e) How long do you have to wait in order to obtain health care for an immediate problem or illness?
 f) How long do you have to wait to obtain health care for an elective procedure such as cosmetic surgery?
 g) In general, how is health care perceived by the people who live in that country?

Option: research paper
Conduct library research to locate four or five articles or books about health care in the country of the person you interviewed for your journal. Make sure that at least two articles or books are from sociology journals or books written by sociologists. Write a paper (around five to seven pages, typed) in which you compare the health-care system in the country you researched with the health-care system in the United States. Describe the way the health care systems in the United States and the other country work. What are the functions and dysfunctions of each? Would the other health-care system work in the United States? What types of changes would occur in our current system? Be sure to provide proper documentation throughout your paper and include a reference page.

ACTIVITY 17. 5

Comparing Different Types Of Healing

Besides the dominant health-care system in the United States made up of physicians, hospitals, nurses, and other supporting staff, there are a variety of other health-care practitioners—such as chiropractors, osteopaths, Christian Science practitioners, mid-wives, acupuncturists, Native American healers and others—that take a different approach to healing. Read about the ones discussed in your introductory textbook.

Journal instructions:
1. Interview three health care practitioners who are not part of the dominant health-care system in the United States, such as those mentioned above. Ask each to discuss what their views on health and illness are, how their views and practices are different from the dominant health-care approach, and some examples of how they would treat various types of illness and disease. Record the interviews with each in your journal.

2. Ask the people you interview for any brochures, pamphlets, or other literature that they may have that describes their approach to health care.

3. Interview a physician who is around forty years of age, one who is around fifty years of age, and one who is around sixty or older. Ask them to respond to and discuss the approaches and views of the above health-care practitioners whom you interviewed.

Option: essay
Write an essay (around five pages, typed) in which you use structural functional, conflict, and symbolic interactionist views on health and illness to

discuss and compare the various types of health care for which you obtained information through your interviews.

Option: research paper

Conduct library research to find four or five articles in sociology journals or books that discuss one of the alternative forms of healing (that is, other than the dominant health-care system) that you discussed in your journal. Write a paper (around five to seven pages, typed) in which you discuss a brief history of that form of healing, the way in which it is practiced and organized, the types of practitioners who are involved, the social context out of which it emerged, the way in which practitioners are socialized into the practice, and so on. Provide proper documentation throughout your paper and include a reference page.

CHAPTER 18

Collective Behavior and Social Movements

One of the central themes in sociology is the notion that many aspects of social reality are not defined absolutely. While most facets of social life are organized and follow rules, there is another dimension that is relatively spontaneous, unstructured, transitory, and unstable. This dimension is often found in the **collective behavior** of groups of people in response to a specific event. Urban riots, stock market crashes, panics, fads, fashions, crazes, and rumors are examples of this type of collective behavior.

Social movements are another type of behavior that reflect a dimension of uncertainty in social life. A social movement is a collective effort to bring about social change and to establish a new order of social thought and action. The pro-democracy movement in Eastern Europe, the women's movement, and the Civil Rights movement are examples of social movements that have challenged previously-defined social orders in American society and throughout the world. These and many other social movements illustrate the idea that the social order consists of agreements about social arrangements - agreements that can be challenged and changed. The existence of social movements such as these are usually perceived as a threat to the dominant groups in society who have obtained their power as a result of the social arrangements that are being challenged.

Because competing groups often disagree about what social arrangements should exist or be maintained, they may try to manipulate public opinion to accept their respective interpretations. This often occurs through **censorship** - prohibiting the distribution of some types of information. By attempting to control the distribution of various types of information—including books, art, movies, news, and so on—groups try to control the public's views about what the social arrangements should be.

ACTIVITY 18. 1

Censorship

Although freedom of the press and speech are guaranteed to Americans by the First Amendment to Constitution, censorship remains a controversial issue in many communities in the United States as well as in many other nations. One way of examining censorship is in terms of the groups that are competing to uphold their respective definitions of social order.

Journal instructions:
1. Look through past issues of national and local newspapers, magazines, and other periodicals to identify two censorship issues that have occurred within the last two years. These can be national issues (such as flag burning, music censorship, art censorship), local issues in your community (such as school books, public art displays), or censorship issues that have occurred in other countries (such as the 1989 Iranian ban on Salman Rushdie's book *The Satanic Verses*). Select issues that are important to you.

2. Look for items in the news in which views about each of these censorship issues are expressed: articles, editorials, essays, letters to the editor, and so on. Try to obtain about ten of these items for each censorship issue you identified. In your journal, provide complete bibliographic data (author, title, source, date, page) and a brief summary of what each author said.

3. Based upon the news items you found, identify the competing groups for each censorship issue, what their positions are, and what you think they are trying to accomplish by their position for or against the censorship in question.

Option: class presentation
Make a five- to ten-minute presentation to your class in which you discuss one of the censorship issues you identified and present arguments for and against it based upon the information you obtained for your journal.

Option: research paper
Conduct library research about one of the censorship issues you selected in your journal. Locate four or five articles from sociology journals, sociology books, commentary magazines, government proceedings, and so forth that you can use to obtain further in-depth information about the censorship issue you selected. Write a paper (five to seven pages, typed) in which you discuss the arguments for and against this censorship. Address questions such as the following: What are the functions and dysfunctions if censorship does and does not take place? Who are the competing groups involved? What definitions of social reality are they trying to maintain with their position?

What are the benefits to each group if they get their way? Provide proper documentation throughout your paper and include a reference page.

ACTIVITY 18. 2

Preconditions Of Collective Behavior

Although collective behavior refers to spontaneous, unstructured, and transitory behavior of groups of people, there are particular conditions that generally precede the collective behavior. These are **structural conduciveness** (the extent to which a social system makes collective behavior possible, such as the presence of various racial groups), **structural strain** (any kind of conflict or ambiguity that causes frustration and stress, such as income inequality), **generalized belief** (the identification of a problem by people and a common interpretation of it, such as racism), **precipitating factors** (an event that triggers a collective response, such as the Rodney King verdict), **mobilization for action** (persuading people to join the movement, such as the call to arms by street gangs), and **the operation of social control** (actions of the mass media, government, or other groups that try to suppress or influence the behavior, such as using the military to suppress collective behavior). Read about the preconditions of collective behavior in your introductory sociology textbook.

Journal instructions:
1. Select an example of collective behavior that occurred within the last two years. Select an example that you witnessed, participated in, knew someone who participated in, or was personally important to you. Locate about ten articles from newspapers, magazines, periodicals, and so forth about this event.

2. Make reference to specific news articles to answer the following questions in your journal about the collective behavior that you identified:
   a) What were were the social structural conditions that were conducive to the collective behavior?
   b) Describe the strains, conflicts, or ambiguities that may have created the stress that preceded the collective behavior.
   c) What beliefs and perceptions about their overall social conditions were held by the people who engaged in the collective behavior?
   d) What specific event triggered the collective behavior?
   e) Were there any attempts by particular groups to promote or instigate the collective behavior? Describe these.
   f) Were there any attempts by authorities or the media to suppress the collective behavior? If so, did these eliminate the collective behavior or did they fuel it?
   g) Could the collective behavior have been anticipated?

3. If possible, interview someone who participated in the collective behavior you identified. If that is not possible, find an interview or discussion from a newspaper or magazine with someone who participated in the behavior. Use the interview to help you answer the above questions.

4. Identify five occupations in which knowledge of the preconditions of collective behavior is important to understand. Briefly discuss how this knowledge could be useful in those occupations.

Option: essay
Write an essay (around three to five pages, typed) in which you discuss the particular example of collective behavior you identified above in terms of the six preconditions of collective behavior.

Option: annotated bibliography
1. Conduct library research to identify ten articles from sociology journals that could offer insights into the type of collective behavior you identified in your journal. These articles do not necessarily have to be about the particular example or type of collective behavior you selected. However, you should select articles that might provide some generalizations about collective behavior that could be used to analyze the example you identified. For example, an article about a race riot might offer some important insights that could be used to help explain a student rebellion at a college, a demonstration by unemployed factory workers, and so on.

2. Read the abstract of each of these articles. Create an annotated bibliography (see Activity 1. 3) in which you list the articles in proper bibliographic style and write one sentence under each listing about how it might be useful in analyzing the collective behavior you identified.

Option: research paper
Use four or more articles from your bibliography and the data you collected in your journal (news articles, interviews, and so on) to write a paper (five to seven pages, typed) in which you discuss the causes of the particular collective behavior you identified and explored in your journal. Be sure to provide proper documentation throughout your paper and include a reference page.

ACTIVITY 18. 3

Theoretical Perspectives On Crowd Behavior

A **crowd** is a collection of people temporarily brought together for some common activity. Sociologists tend to classify crowds into four types: a

137

casual crowd (a nonemotional, unstructured crowd such as people gathering on a corner to watch an accident or a street musician); a **conventional crowd** (a crowd of people who have intentionally gathered at an event for a common purpose that is governed by specific norms, such as a religious ceremony or a sporting event); an **expressive crowd** (a crowd with no immediate purpose other than the release of tension or expression of emotion, such as people in the throes of a religious experience or overcome by the music at a rock concert); and an **acting crowd** (a crowd that has a focus that is addressed by acting outside the norms, such as a mob or a riot) (Blumer, 1978).

While some types of crowd behavior are purely spontaneous and the result of people simply being in the same place at the same time, other types are the result of social forces that shape the behavior of the people. The **classical perspectives , interactionist perspective, emergent norm perspective,** and **game perspective** offer various explanations of the forces that shape crowds. Read about these theories in your introductory sociology text.

Journal instructions:
1. In your journal, use each of the above theories of crowd behavior (or the ones that are discussed in your introductory sociology book) as guides to develop a list of things to look for if you want to use a sociological perspective to explain the way a crowd acts. For example, guided by the emergent norm perspective, you might look to see if there are any norms that develop within a crowd, examine how they develop, and note how they influence the behavior of the crowd.

2. Observe three events in which large crowds are present; for example, a football game, a homecoming parade, a rock concert, a religious revival (or watch a evangelical television program), a lecture, a strike, a demonstration, a rally, and so on.
   a) Indicate what each type of crowd each one is (casual, conventional, expressive, or acting) and the observations that led you to label them as such.
   b) Use the list of items you developed above as a guide to observe the behavior of each of the people in each of the events. Note your observations in your journal.

3. Briefly discuss which theory you think is most appropriate to describe each type of crowd you observed. For example, after observing a religious revival in which many people are caught in the throes of a conversion (expressive crowd), you might decide that social contagion theory (interactionist perspective) is an appropriate way to explain an expressive crowd behavior. Discuss what leads you to your conclusion. There may be more than one theory that adequately explains each type of crowd behavior. Discuss all the ones you think are relevant.

4. Identify one occupation for each type of crowd (casual, conventional, expressive, or acting) in which understanding how and why crowds behave the way they do might be helpful (for example, clergyperson, police officer, military officer, concert organizer, commercial artist, and so on).

5. Select one theory of crowd behavior that might provide useful knowledge in each of these occupations and explain why. (For example, which theory would be most useful for organizers of political rallies?)

ACTIVITY 18. 4

Social Movements

A **social movement** is a long-term collective conscious effort to bring about social change or to prevent social change. There are hundreds of examples of social movements throughout the United States and other countries, such as the civil rights movement, the peace movement, the ecology movement, the gay liberation movement, the nuclear freeze movement, the women's movement, and many others. A social movement is distinguished from collective behavior in that it is a conscious, long-term, well-planned effort whereas collective behavior generally refers to relatively spontaneous, unstructured, transitory behavior.

Social movements are classified in many different ways by many different sociologists. Social movements have been classified as **value-oriented, power-oriented, participant-oriented, reactionary, conservative, resistant, reformist, revolutionary, nationalistic, utopian, religious,** and **expressive.**

Journal instructions:
1. Read about the types of social movements that are explained and discussed in your introductory sociology textbook. List them in your journal and briefly define them.

2. Look through recent and past issues of newspapers and magazines to identify examples of four types of social movements that your book discusses that are currently underway in the United States or in another country. Make sure at least one of the social movements you identify has a presence or is active in the area where you live; or make sure that can identify at least one person affiliated with one of the social movements whom you will be able to interview and use as a source of information about the movement. Once you look, you will find an abundance of social movements that have a presence in your area and people affiliated with one or another social movement: faculty members, students, neighbors, politicians, and so on.

139

3. Obtain at least five newspaper and/or news magazine articles about <u>each</u> of these movements. Use these articles to discuss the following in your journal:

a) Explain how you defined each example as a particular type of movement.

b) Describe the social change that each movement is trying to encourage or discourage.

c) Discuss who the leaders (individuals and/or groups) of each movement are.

d) Discuss the types of tactics that the leaders and/or members of each movement use to try to obtain their goals.

Option: essay

1. Attend a rally, meeting, lecture, or other gathering of people who are involved with one of the social movements and/or contact a person who is actively involved in one of the social movements you identified in your journal. From the meeting you attend or person you contact, obtain pamphlets, brochures, magazines, books, or other literature they may have available for you to borrow. Use your observations of a meeting, your contact person, and the literature you obtain, to help you answer items in question three (above).

2. Interview a person who is involved in the movement and ask him or her to discuss:

a) what the movement is about;

b) why he or she is involved in it;

c) what it is like to be part of this movement;

d) how the movement hopes to accomplish its goals;

e) if they think the movement will be successful.

3. Write an essay (around five pages, typed) in which you use sociological theories from the chapter on social movements in your text to discuss the social movement you selected in terms of the above questions.

Option: research paper

1. Read about the stages of development of social movements in your introductory sociology text (**social unrest, popular excitement, formalization,** and **institutionalization**).

2. Conduct library research about one of the social movements you identified in your journal activity. Obtain five articles from sociology journals and/or sociology books about social movements. Use your library's indexes (*Sociological Abstracts, Social Science Index,* and so on) and the list of suggested readings at the end of the social movements chapter in your introductory text for some ideas.

3. Write a paper (around five to seven pages, typed) in which you use your library research and the information you collected in your journal to discuss the stages of development of this movement. Provide proper documentation throughout your paper and include a reference page.

ACTIVITY 18. 5

Public Opinion

Public opinion—the opinion held by a substantial number of people or the dominant opinion in a given population - can be a very powerful force in societies. They can help to determine what social, political, and economic policies become accepted, which politicians become elected, the types of products that are sold by businesses, and so forth. Public opinion is usually measured through a survey known as a **public opinion poll.** Since public opinion can be a very powerful force in society, groups who have a particular goal that they want to achieve may attempt to manipulate public opinion through the use of **propaganda.** Propaganda often is used to shape public opinion in order to meet the goals of business, government, religions, and other groups in society.

Journal instructions:
1. Look through issues of newspapers (national and local) and news magazines for the past month to find four or five reports on public opinion about important social issues or events and examples of how various groups use propaganda to try to influence public opinion. Describe these in your journal.

2. Select one issue or event on which you can trace the reports on public opinion for three to six months. For example, you might look at how public opinion about approval ratings of the President of the United States, about attitudes toward controversial policies such as abortion or sex education, and so on. Note the extent to which public opinion has changed or stayed the same during the time period you select. See if you can identify the ways in which particular groups have tried to manipulate public opinion on this item and describe them in your journal.

3. Identify and discuss in your journal three occupations in which knowledge about public opinion and how it is influenced might be useful.

CHAPTER 19

Population and Ecology

One of the most concrete, practical, and useful areas of sociology is **demography**—the study of the size and makeup (that is, age, gender, race, ethnicity, and so on) of the human population and how it changes. The size and makeup of the population has important consequences for societies. Therefore, sociological knowledge about populations is important and useful for a variety of reasons.

Understanding the demographic trends of a society—such as rates of birth, death, fertility, and migration—are important in helping community planners and policy makers assess the future needs of communities and societies. Community planners and policy makers must take into consideration the demographic characteristics of the present and future population in order to meet important social needs such as housing, education, transportation, health care, child care, elderly care, recreation, and others.

Businesses must consider demographic trends in their advertising and marketing strategies, in their research and development, and in determining what types of goods and services will be needed by consumers in the coming years. For example, it could be crucial to the long-term growth of the automobile industry to understand that the median age of the population is increasing. Do middle-aged people with families want two-door coupes, with large engines, and small back seats, or are they more likely to want station wagons? Is the increasing age of the population likely to help the restaurant industry or hurt it? What are the implications for the clothing industry as the age of the population increases? There are innumerable ways in which population characteristics must be considered by businesses.

Population trends are an important factor in environmental pollution and the depletion of natural resources. While the causes of environmental pollution and resource depletion are complex and varied, they are clearly affected by a rapidly increasing worldwide population.

Finally, our personal lives are affected by population trends. Opportunities for employment, education, housing, marriage, and other human needs are affected by population characteristics. Social issues related to population trends may affect our personal lives. For example, how will the Social Security system be affected when it is burdened with an extremely large population of people over 65 years of age? How will housing investments be affected as the number of home-buying-aged people increases or decreases?

Clearly, it is important for all of us to have a knowledge of the ways in which population affects society.

ACTIVITY 19. 1

Occupational Uses Of Demographic Analysis

As suggested above, demographic analysis is important in a number of occupations within government, private business, and non-profit organizations. There are many opportunities for people who have the skills to design studies, analyze data, make forecasts, and prepare reports about population trends.

Journal instructions:
1. Identify two or three occupations in each of the above employment sectors (government, private business, non-profit organizations) in which population trends need to be considered. Some examples are city managers and county commissioners (government); advertisers, marketing directors, and insurance agents (private business); school superintendents and social service agency directors (non-profit organizations). There are many other examples. To help you arrive at some other examples, talk to the job placement counselor in your college, a personnel officer at a business, a person who works at an employment agency, a person who works for the local government, or anyone who works in any of the above employment sectors.

2. For each of the occupations you identified (you should have a total of six to nine), briefly describe in your journal how knowledge of population trends is important.

3. Locate one person from each of the employment sectors for which you identified occupations. Ask each of these three people the following questions and record their responses in your journal:
   a) How important is knowledge of population trends in your work?
   b) What specific types of information do you need to know about the population and why?
   c) How do you go about obtaining this information?

d) What are some issues or problems that you are currently facing or have had to deal with recently that are related to population trends?

e) What are some specific policies that were created in your organization that involved knowledge of the population?

4. Go to your college library and ask your reference librarian to provide you with a list or show you the different sources of population data that your library has. Examine each of these sources or references and discuss, in your journal, which ones would be useful for each of the three occupations you selected above.

Option: essay

Read the chapter on population in your introductory sociology textbook. Pick out all of the concepts, theories, and facts that you think would be important in helping the three people you interviewed in their work. Write an essay (around three to five pages, typed) in which you discuss the uses of demographic analysis in the workplace, using the occupations of the three people you interviewed as examples throughout the paper. Discuss specifically how each of the concepts, theories, and facts you selected from the chapter could be useful within these occupations.

ACTIVITY 19. 2

Using The Census At Work

The **census**, or a count of the population, can be useful in many areas of work. In the United States, a national census has been carried out every ten years since 1790. In the ten-year census, every household must answer a questionnaire. A smaller census is carried out every year that is based upon a random sample of households. In addition to population counts, the census is a record of **vital statistics**—births, deaths and their causes, marriages, divorces, some diseases, and other similar data.

Journal instructions:

1. Think of five occupations in which using census data might be useful. In your journal, write about how census data could be useful in each of these occupations.

2. Locate the most current ten-year and yearly United States census in your library (U.S. Bureau of the Census, *Statistical Abstract of the United States*). Identify all the types of information contained within the census that could be helpful in each of the five occupations you listed above and discuss how.

Option: essay
Select one of the occupations you listed above and the census data that you found that would be useful in that occupation. Trace how these items have changed during the last ten years. Write a three- to five-page essay in which you discuss how these changes might have affected the way people in that occupation work, the goals or objectives of the occupation, the nature of the problems that people in it might encounter, and other population changes that you think are relevant to that occupation.

ACTIVITY 19. 3

How Fertility, Mortality, and Migration Affect Populations

Fertility is a measure of the rate at which people are born. **Mortality** is a measure of the rate at which people die. **Migration** is the movement of people into or out of a geographical area. These factors can have significant impacts upon the welfare and types of problems that countries may face. Go to your introductory sociology textbook and read about how these three factors can influence the types of issues and problems that societies face.

Journal instructions:
1. Look through newspapers and news magazines for the past year to identify five to ten issues and problems (such as starvation, overpopulation, spread of disease, unemployment, and so on) in various countries throughout the world that are the result of a country's fertility, mortality, or migration rates.

2. In your journal, describe these issues and problems and briefly discuss what each of the countries is doing to try to cope with them. That is, what policies have they undertaken or are they considering that might help them deal with these issues or problems?

Option: research paper
Select one of the countries that you discussed in your journal that faces problems or issues related to mortality, fertility, or migration. Locate four or five articles in sociology journals or books that discuss the causes and effects of demographic changes in that country. (Use the *Social Science Index*, *Sociological Abstracts,* and other indexes to help you find articles. Look in *Contemporary Sociology* for reviews of books on these topics.) Write a paper (around five pages, typed) in which you discuss how mortality, fertility, and migration rates have affected that country's issues and problems now and in the past and the types of policies that have been enacted to deal with these issues and problems. Be sure to provide proper documentation throughout your paper and include a reference page.

ACTIVITY 19. 4

How Population Trends Affect Your Life

A **population pyramid** is a graphic representation of how many males and females from each age category there are in a particular country. Population pyramids enable us to see what percentage of people are of each age and gender at a given time. The percentage of the population that is your age can have important effects on many areas of your life: mate selection, educational opportunities, cost of education, job opportunities, cost of housing, and many others. Go to your introductory sociology text and read the section on how population trends are related to life experiences.

Journal instructions:
1. Locate a population pyramid of the United States that includes your age group. Many introductory sociology texts may have examples of them (for example, Eshleman et al, 1993; Thio, 1992; Hess et al, 1991; and others. Or, you can find one in Population Reference Bureau's *Statistical Abstract of the United States*, 1991, p. 16.).

2. Find the year in which you were born on the pyramid. Look at the percentage of people of your age and of each gender in comparison to people older and younger than you. In your journal, list and discuss all the ways in which the size and composition of people in your age group might affect your opportunities and lifestyles (for example, educational, housing, marital, cost of living, and others.) After you do this for yourself, compare your age and gender group with your parents' and grandparents' groups and how their opportunities and lifestyles were affected by population characteristics. (For further ideas as to how you can use a population pyramid to examine your opportunities, see Kennedy, 1986, chapter 2.)

Option: essay
Write a paper (around five pages, typed) in which you use examples from your journal to discuss the impact of population trends on life experiences.

ACTIVITY 19. 5

Environment

Besides being of interest to sociologists, the environment has become one of the most controversial political topics of this decade. While not the only reason, the increasing worldwide population is partially responsible for environmental problems. Political positions about the environment are varied. Some feel that stricter policies should be enforced that would regulate consumer and industrial behavior; others feel that regulation is unnecessary and will hurt the economy. This is not an issue that concerns just the United States, but concerns all countries around the world.

Journal instructions:
1. Look through the indexes in your library (*Reader's Guide to Periodical Literature, Social Science Index,* and others) to help you find newspaper or magazine articles about ten environmental issues, problems, or policy debates that have appeared in the news within the past year. Discuss each of these in your journal.

2. In your journal, categorize these issues or problems in terms of types. Develop whatever categories you think will work to help you do this (for example, industrial pollution, consumer pollution, water pollution, and so on). Then discuss what you see as the main reasons for each type of environmental problem.

Option: research paper
1. One very controversial debate concerning the environment is whether there should be stricter environmental protection measures on consumer and industrial behavior than currently exist. There have been many arguments for and against strict environmental protection measures. Conduct library research to locate arguments for and against these stricter measures. Use a variety of your libraries indexes and reference material to help you do this (for example, *Reader's Guide to Periodical Literature, Social Science Index, Newsbank, New York Times Index,* and many others). You should locate a few articles or books written by sociologists, but you do not have to confine yourself to these. Textbooks on social problems (for example, Currie and Skolnick, 1988; Neubeck, 1991; Parillo et al., 1989) might also be useful.

2. Write a paper (around five pages, typed) in which you:
   a) Introduce the debate about environmental protection and provide some examples of measures that have been suggested by various political groups.
   b) Present <u>balanced</u> arguments for <u>and</u> against stricter environmental protection measures.
   c) Take a position for <u>or</u> against stricter environmental protection measures. In taking your position, use material from your library research <u>and</u> sociological theories (such as structural functionalism, conflict theory, or others) that might be relevant. You may need to go back and read about these theories in the chapters on theory, social stratification, political systems, and economic systems.

Provide proper documentation throughout your paper and include a reference page.

CHAPTER 20

The Changing Community

A persistent problem that has plagued communities as far back as the Middle Ages in Europe and at least to the colonial era in America is homelessness (Schutt, 1990; Wright, 1989). However, the nature and magnitude of homelessness in America has changed dramatically during the past few decades. For example, when compared with a few decades ago, today's homeless are increasing in number, suffer a more severe housing deprivation, are increasingly higher percentages of women and children, are much younger, have greater economic hardships, are increasingly members of racial and ethnic groups, and are less likely to be alcohol and drug abusers (Eshleman et al, 1993, p. 529).

Sociologists are particularly interested in explaining the persistence and growth of homelessness and in debunking the myths about the homeless. Some of the more common myths are that people are homeless because they are mentally impaired, alcoholics and/or other drug abusers, and lazy, and that they have a choice about their homeless condition. As James Wright states, "Some of the homeless *are* broken-down alcoholics, but most are not. Some *are* mentally impaired, but most are not. Some *are* living off the benefit programs made available through the social welfare system, but most are not" (Wright, 1989, p. 46). There are a number of interrelated and complex reasons for homelessness today that go beyond the popular stereotypes about the homeless and that have been addressed in many books and articles written for sociologists and other social scientists (see, for example, Schutt, 1990). Most agree that the most basic reasons for homelessness today include an insufficient supply of affordable of housing, an increase in the poverty rate, a deterioration of the purchasing power of welfare benefits, and a decrease in social supports to help the poor establish themselves (Schutt, 1990; Wright, 1989).

The issue of homelessness is relevant to many areas of sociology - for example, social stratification, political systems, economic systems, and minority groups. However, it is particularly relevant to the sociological study

148

of communities because the growth and change of urban communities are partially responsible for homelessness.

ACTIVITY 20. 1

Homelessness

As mentioned above, there are many myths about homeless people. However, when we look at the facts we see that many of these myths have no basis.

Journal instructions:
1. Interview five people who are not experts in understanding the nature of homelessness. For example, interview some of your friends, your parents, neighbors, and so on. Ask them the following and record their answers in your journal:
   a) Do you personally know anyone who is homeless, that is, who sleeps on the streets, in a homeless shelter, in a car, or somewhere else besides a home?
   b) Why do you think that <u>most</u> people who are homeless are so?
   c) What do you think are some typical characteristics of homeless people?
   d) Do you think that all people could find a place to live if they really wanted to?

2. Find four or five articles, essays, or letters to the editor about homelessness that have appeared in newspapers or newsmagazines during the past year. In your journal, summarize the views about homelessness portrayed in the articles, essays, or letters.

3. Visit a homeless shelter in your area. Observe it for one or two hours on three separate occasions and at different times of the day (morning, midday, and night). Talk to as many of the people there as you can. Ask them why they are there and what conditions led them to become homeless. Also, talk to the director of the homeless shelter. Ask the director if homelessness is increasing in the area and the reasons for the increase or decrease in homelessness. Record these discussions in your journal.

4. In your journal, compare the views of the people you first interviewed about homeless people, the views you found in the newspapers, and your observations and discussions at the homeless shelter.

Option: essay
Write an essay (around five pages, typed) in which you discuss popular conceptions about homelessness with the realities of homelessness that you observed. Reread the sections on life chances and theories of inequality in the chapter on social stratification in your introductory sociology text. Incorporate some of this information into your essay.

Option: research paper
1. Conduct library research to find four or five articles in sociology journals or books that discuss the extent of homelessness in the United States today and the reasons for it (for example, Eshleman et al, 1993; Schutt, 1990; Wright, 1989; Rossi, 1989; Neubeck, 1991; and many others).

2. Write a paper (around five to seven pages, typed) in which you discuss the nature of homelessness today and the reasons for it. Provide proper documentation throughout your paper and include a reference page.

ACTIVITY 20. 2

Examining Urban Structure

There are a variety of models developed by sociologists to describe **urban ecology** - the spatial arrangement of cities and the processes that create and reinforce these arrangements. Three of the most well-known are the **concentric zone model** developed by Ernest W. Burgess (1925), the **sector model** developed by Homer Hoyt (1939), and the **multiple-nuclei model** developed by Chauncy Harris and Edward Ullman (1945). Go to your introductory sociology textbook and study these models.

Journal instructions:
1. In your journal, briefly summarize in your own words and provide a diagram of each of the above models of urban space.

2. Obtain a street map and a census map of the city or county in which you live or are currently residing. Call the city or county offices, look in the city library, or talk to someone who works at the Chamber of Commerce to help you obtain these maps.

3. Using these maps, determine which, if any, of the above ecological models seems to fit your area. You may have to become more familiar with the area to do this. Here are some things that you might try to do to become more familiar with the area. You do not necessarily have to do any or all of them (but be sure to keep a record of the ones you do). Do the ones that are possible for you and will provide you with the information you need to determine the appropriate model:
    a) Spend a few hours driving through different parts of the city noting the ecological patterns of industry, shopping areas, residential areas, and so on.
    b) Talk to a city planner or a member of the Chamber of Commerce who is very familiar with the ecology of the area.
    c) Try to obtain access to an aerial photographic map of the area. There is probably one in your municipal office building that you can look at.

4. In your journal, discuss which ecological model seems to fit and why. If none of the above models seem to fit, develop your own model for the area and explain it.

5. Find out why the ecological pattern in your area developed the way it did. To do this you may have to interview a member of the city government or someone who works at the Chamber of Commerce. Try to obtain access to any records, photographs, documents, or other data that may help you understand the area's ecological development. In your journal, discuss the reasons for the area's ecological development.

6.   Based upon what you have found out about your city's ecological development and current trends, discuss in your journal how you think its ecology will change within the next ten to twenty years. Who will be affected most by these changes?

Option: research paper
Conduct library research to locate four or five sociology journal articles and/or books that discuss models of urban ecology. Write an paper (around five to seven pages, typed) in which you discuss your area's ecological development and the prospects for the future by using the information you obtained in your journal and ideas found from your library research. Provide proper documentation throughout your paper and include a reference page.

ACTIVITY 20. 3

Gemeinschaft Or *Gesellschaft*: **How Community Type Affects Our Lives**

The German sociologist Ferdinand Tonnies (1887) made a distinction between different types of communities, how they are organized, and their effects upon the way people live. A *gemeinschaft* community is characterized by primary relationships—personal, deep, extensive, emotional, and collectively oriented. A *gesellschaft* community is characterized b y secondary relationships—impersonal, instrumental, rational, and self-oriented. Go to your introductory sociology text and read about *gemeinschaft* and *gesellschaft* communities.

Journal instructions:
1. Identify the type of community in which you live as either a *gemeinschaft* or a *gesellschaft*. For one full day, carry your journal with you everywhere you go and write extensive notes describing examples of things you observe that are characteristic of the type of community you identified. For example, observe relationships between people at work, in stores, in the doctor's office,

between pedestrians, at the dentist, at the post office, between neighbors, and so on.

2. Identify a community near where you live that is the opposite of the type of community in which you live. Spend a half a day in that community observing relationships between people in similar situations as you observed above (at work, in stores, at the post office, in a doctor's office, and so on). Keep extensive notes of your observations in your journal.

3. Briefly discuss the different features of each of the communities that you observed and provide some reasons why people act toward each other the way they do in each of them.

Option: essay
Write an essay (around four to five pages) in which you discuss the two communities that you observed in terms of their *gemeinschaft* and *gesellschaft* characteristics and how each type of community seemed to affect the way people lived in each. Provide extensive examples.

Option: research paper
1. Conduct library research in order to locate an article from a sociology journal or book that is a community study of a *gemeinschaft* and one that is a community study of a *gesellschaft*. There are many. Some good places to look for such an article or book would be in the *Sociological Abstracts* or *Contemporary Sociology* under the heading of community studies or urban sociology. It is not likely that the title of the article or book will contain the words *"gemeinschaft"* or *"gesellschaft,"* but you should be able to get an idea from the title about the type of community that is discussed.

2. Write a paper (around five pages, typed) in which you compare the two communities you read about in terms of their *gemeinschaft* or *gesellschaft* characteristics. Provide proper documentation throughout your paper and include a reference page.

ACTIVITY 20. 4

Assessing Urban Issues, Problems, And Needs

There are numerous issues and problems faced by urban areas: poverty, unemployment, crime, pollution, waste disposal, water purity, transportation, housing, population congestion, and so on. Rural and suburban areas may face some of these problems also, but usually not to the extent that urban areas do. In order to deal with issues and help solve problems, it is important first to be able to determine what they are and if it is possible to solve them.

Journal instructions:
1. Select an urban area near where you live. Identify, and discuss in your journal, what you think are the five most important problems and issues that that area has had to deal with during the last few years. In order to find this information out, you should:
    a) Do a content analysis of articles, news stories, essays, letters to the editor, and other news items about urban issues and problems that have appeared in the area newspaper during the past few years.
    b) Interview people from law enforcement, social service, and community service agencies to obtain data about crime, poverty, unemployment, drug abuse, homelessness, or other problems and issues.
    c) Talk with people who live and work in the area to find out what they think some of the most important issues and problems are.
    d) Interview a city government official or city planner to find out some of the most important issues and problems that the city government has had to deal with during the past few years. Ask the person you interview what is being done, either by the city or by private organizations, to help deal with these issues and problems. Also, find out if there are any public or private resources with which to deal with these issues and problems.

Option: essay
Pretend that you have been hired as a consultant by the urban area you studied above in order to determine what some of the major issues and problems are, what types of resources are available to deal with them, and what you would recommend to help solve the problems. Present your ideas in an essay (around five pages, typed) based upon the information you collected for your journal and ideas found within the chapter on urban communities in your introductory sociology text.

Option: research paper
Select one of the urban issues and problems that you identified in your journal. Find four or five articles in sociology journals and/or sociology books that discuss research conducted about this type of issue or problem. Write a paper (around five to seven pages, typed) in which you use sociological ideas, theories, and research findings from these articles to discuss why the problem you selected exists and what might be done to deal with it.

ACTIVITY 20. 5

Urban Planning

Sociological knowledge plays an important part in urban planning. Some sociologists and other social scientists (such as political scientists, public administrators, geographers, and historians) have jobs in urban planning as consultants and researchers for state, city, and local governments and for engineers, architects, lawyers, and others involved in planning cities and communities.

Journal instructions:

1. Identify someone who works in city management, city government, or city planning. If you do not know anyone who is employed in this type of work, ask a public administration professor at your college, or go to the city office building in the area where you live to ask for some suggestions of someone who works in city planning with whom you can talk. Conduct an interview with the person in order to find out about the type of work he or she does. What type of training or education does the person have? What is a typical workday like? What are some important issues and problems the city faces? What are some projects that are currently being worked on? What types of future projects for the city are currently planned or in the planning stages? Record this information in your journal.

2. Ask the person you interview if you can talk with and observe other city planners at work for a few hours one day. If possible, ask the people you meet the same types of questions as above.

3. Find theories, ideas, concepts, data, and so on in the chapter on urban communities in your introductory sociology text that you think might be useful in helping city planners do their job.

Option: essay

Write an essay (around three to five pages, typed) in which you discuss the type of work that city planners in your area do, examples of projects currently being worked on, the type of professional training or educational training they have, and how sociological knowledge can be useful in their work.

CHAPTER 21

The Nature of Social Change

One of the most exciting aspects of sociology to those who study and practice it is its focus on contemporary issues. In a rapidly changing world such as ours, many of these contemporary issues have to do with the impact of social change on the structure of societies and their institutions. Think of the changes that have occured in your lifetime alone: the demise of communism in the former Soviet Union and other Eastern European countries, the dismantling of the Berlin Wall, the proliferation of computers in our daily lives, vast swings in the U.S. and worldwide economy, significant changes in gender roles in the family and in the workplace, and many other examples that have been discussed in your introductory sociology textbook.

However, rapid social change is not new. Sociology developed partly in response to rapid social changes that were occuring during the Industrial Revolution. Early sociologists wanted to know whether the social change that was occuring as a result of the Industrial Revolution was good or bad, and what the effects on social life might be. As traditions rapidly vanished and changed, the vision of the future was not as secure as it once had been.

Today, sociologists accept social change as a natural part of social life, but are still interested in the reasons for it and the impact on people when their society changes. Whether or not you are a sociologist, understanding the impact of social change on peoples' lives is important.

ACTIVITY 21. 1

Changes In Eastern Europe

Since the late 1980s, rapid changes have been taking place in Eastern Europe. Dramatic shifts in political, economic, and social systems have occured in Hungary, Poland, Germany, Czechoslovakia, the former Yugoslavia, and in almost every country in Eastern Europe. Unsurprisingly, much of the Western world has reacted positively to these changes, especially the demise of the communist party in the former Soviet Union. What many Westerners perceived as an oppressive system appeared to give way to a free system. However positive these changes may appear, though, people often overlook their full impact on individuals, society, and culture.

Journal instructions:
1. Select one of the countries of Eastern Europe that has undergone significant changes in its political and economic systems within the last five years, such as East Germany or countries of the former Soviet Union. Find five articles, essays, or editorials that appeared in newspapers or magazines around the time that the changes were occurring. In your journal, summarize the views and opinions expressed in these articles.

2. Find five news items that discuss how the country you selected has fared one to two years (or more) after the changes occurred. For example, how have people's lives changed? Is life better or worse? What are some new problems that the society faces? And so on. Discuss these in your journal.

3. If possible, interview someone on your campus who is from the country that you selected (for example, a foreign exchange student, a visiting professor, or any one else from the country). Ask the person to describe what life was like for him/her before and after the changes occurred.

4. Interview a political science professor or sociology professor on your campus who studies international affairs or a politician who is involved in international affairs. Ask him or her what their views are on what the impact of the changes in this country have been and are likely to be on the institutions, culture, and lives of the people who live there.

5. Reread the chapters on culture and social change in your introductory sociology textbook. In your journal, discuss the impact of the changes that have occurred on the culture of that country.

6. Identify two occupations in which knowledge about how social change affects culture and society can be useful and discuss how.

Option: class presentation
Prepare a ten-minute presentation that you will make to your class in which you discuss how knowledge of the social changes that occurred in the country you described, and sociological knowledge that explains those changes, could be useful in three different occupations.

Option: essay
Write an essay (around five pages, typed) in which you use the theories and concepts about social change explained in your introductory sociology textbook to discuss the changes that have occurred in the country you described in your journal.

Option: research paper
Conduct library research to locate three to five articles in sociology journals that discuss the changes that have occurred in the country you wrote about in your journal. Write a paper (around five to seven pages, typed) in which you use the ideas found within the journal articles to help you explain the changes that you described in your journal. Provide proper documentation throughout your paper and include a reference page.

ACTIVITY 21. 2

Should the United States Provide Economic Assistance To The Former Soviet Republics?

The changes in Eastern Europe—particularly in the former Soviet Union—do not affect only the countries there. The social, political, and economic changes will have an impact on countries in the West. Therefore, there has been much debate over whether the United States and other Western nations should provide—or continue to provide—economic assistance to the former Soviet Republics. This has been discussed in the popular media, as well as in government and academic circles.

Research paper:
1. Use your library's indexes and reference material (*Reader's Guide to Periodical Literature, Social Science Index, New York Times Index*, and others) to find five articles or essays that support providing economic aid to the former Soviet Republics and five articles that oppose providing economic aid.

2. Read the chapters on social change, economic systems, and political systems in your introductory sociology textbook. Write a paper (around five to seven pages, typed) in which you:
   a) Introduce the issue of economic aid to the former Soviet Republics (and other Eastern nations that have changed their political and economic systems) and why it is important.
   b) Discuss three reasons why the United States should provide economic assistance.
   c) Discuss three reasons why the United States should not provide economic assistance.

d)   Use sociological theories and/or concepts (from your textbook's chapters on economic systems, political systems, and/or social change) to take a position on this issue. That is, after you present balanced arguments for and against economic aid, decide which position you favor and use sociological ideas to support it.

Provide proper documentation throughout your paper and include a reference page.

ACTIVITY 21. 3

The Impact of Discoveries And Inventions

A **discovery** is the act of finding something that has always existed but that no one previously knew about. An **invention** is a device constructed by putting two or more things together in a new way. Discoveries and inventions are called **innovations**, changes that offer something new to society and that alter its norms or institutions. **Diffusion** is the process by which an innovation is spread throughout a social system. Rapid diffusion can have significant effects on the way we live our lives.

Journal instructions:
1. Think about, identify, and list in your journal the major innovations that have become widely diffused through American society and/or other societies within the last ten years; for example, personal computers, cellular telephones, camcorders, and so on. For one week, carefully observe the ways in which the innovations you identified are used by people in their everyday lives. Keep your journal with you at all times—in school, at work, during leisure time, and so on—and keep a detailed record of your observations.

2. After each observation, write a few comments about how you think the innovation(s) has affected the behavior and lifestyle of the person using it, and cultural norms, values, and beliefs. For example, suppose you see someone talking on their cellular telephone while driving on the highway. Discuss how the cellular telephone likely has affected their family life, work life, leisure time, and so on. How has it affected norms, values, and beliefs regarding work, the family, leisure time, and so on? Feel free to speculate and be creative. At the end of one week you should have dozens of examples.

Option: research paper
1. Select one of the innovations that you identified above. Look through the *Reader's Guide to Periodical Literature*, the *Social Science Index*, *Sociological Abstracts, Newsbank,* and other indexes in your library to identify at least five articles in newspapers or news magazines, commentary

magazines, or sociology journals that discuss the impact of that innovation on people's lives and how it might change people's lives in the future. Make sure that at least one of the articles is from a sociology journal. Locate and read the articles.

2. Write a paper (around five pages, typed) in which you discuss how the innovation you selected has already affected social values, norms, lifestyles, and institutions and what the implications are for the future. Provide proper documentation throughout your paper and include a reference page.

ACTIVITY 21. 4

Theories of Modernization of Underdeveloped Countries

While much of the sociological study of social change examines the changes that have occurred and continue to occur in the modernized, industrial nations of the world, it has become increasingly important to be able to understand changes that are occurring in underdeveloped nations. There are two theoretical viewpoints regarding this type of change: **modernization theory and world systems (or dependency) theory.** These are important theories for you to understand. Go to your introductory sociology textbook and study the section in the chapter on social change that describes these theories.

Journal and research paper:
1. In your journal, summarize, in your own words, the viewpoints of modernization theory and world systems theory.

2. Identify one Third World (or underdeveloped) nation that has been undergoing changes during the last ten years. Find articles that appeared in newspapers and magazines during the past ten years (at least one article per year) that discuss some of the changes that have occurred in the country you identified.

3. Locate two articles in sociology journals or two sociology books that discuss changes in underdeveloped nations. There are many. For articles in sociology journals, check the *Social Science Index* or the *Sociological Abstracts*. For books, check the journal *Contemporary Sociology*. In your journal, discuss the explanations that these articles or books offer about the types of change that has been occurring in Third World nations.

4. Write a paper (around five to seven pages, typed) in which you do the following:
   a) Introduce the topic of change in the Third World nation you selected.

159

b) Discuss some of the changes that have occurred in that country during the past ten years.

c) Use some of the ideas from the sociology articles or books that you found to help you explain some of the changes that have occurred.

d) Discuss the changes in that country in terms of modernization or world systems theory, depending upon which one you feel is most applicable.

Provide proper documentation throughout your paper and include a reference page.

ACTIVITY 21. 5

Social Change And You

Social change affects us in many ways. Changes in the size of the population, gender roles, fertility and mortality, economic systems, political systems, and many other aspects of social life impact not only society, but also our individual lives.

Journal instructions:

1. In various chapters of your introductory sociology textbook you will find tables or figures that examine changes in some aspect of society over different time periods - divorce rates, number of women in the workplace, income inequality between rich and poor, and many others. Go through each chapter of your introductory textbook and find all of the tables, figures, and discussions that illustrate changes over time that have occurred in U.S. and other societies throughout the world.

2. In your journal, summarize what each of these tables and figures is about, the type of change indicated by each, and what the impact of this change might be on individuals' lives. Write about a paragraph for each.

Option: essay

Write a paper (around five pages, typed) in which you use the above material to discuss how changes in U.S. society and around the world will make your life different than your parents' and your grandparents' lives.

REFERENCES

Adler, Jerry, Mark Starr, Farai Chideya, Lynda Wright, Pat Wingert, and Linda Haac. 1990. "Taking Offense: Is This the New Enlightenment on Campus or the New McCarthyism?" *Newsweek*, (December 24): 48-54.

Aho, James A. 1991. *The Politics of Righteousness: Idaho Christian Patriotism*. Seattle: University of Washington Press.

Ammerman, Nancy Tatom. 1990. *Baptist Battles: Social Change and Religious Conflict in the Southern Baptist Convention*. N.J.: Rutgers University Press.

Ashley, David and David Michael Orenstein. 1990. *Sociological Theory: Classical Statements*, 2d edition. Boston: Allyn and Bacon, Inc.

Babbie, Earl. 1992. *The Practice of Social Research*. 6th edition. Belmont, California: Wadsworth Publishing Company.

Becker, Howard S. 1967. "Whose Side Are We On?." *Social Problems* 14: 239-47.

Belsky, Jay. 1990. "Infant Day Care, Child Development, and Family Policy." *Society* 27 (July/August): 10-12.

Bernstein, Richard. 1990. "In U.S. Schools: A War of Words," *New York Times Magazine*. (October 14): 34.

Blumer, Herbert. 1939. "Collective Behavior," in Alfred McClung Lee, ed. *Principles of Sociology*. New York: Barnes and Noble.

Browne-Miller, Angela. 1990. *The Day Care Dilemma: Critical Concerns for American Families*. New York: Plenum Press.

Burgess, Ernest. 1925. "The Growth of the City." in Robert E. Park and Ernest Burgess, eds., *The City*. Chicago: University of Chicago Press: 47-62.

Clark, Candace, and Howard Robboy, editors. 1988. *Social Interaction: Readings in Sociology*, 3rd edition, New York: St. Martin's Press.

Clarke-Stewart, K. Alison. "Infant Day Care: Maligned or Malignant?." *American Psychologist* 44 (February): 266-73.

Collins, Randall. 1985. *Three Sociological Traditions*. New York: Oxford University Press.

Collins, Randall and Michael Makowsky. 1988. *The Discovery of Society*. 4th edition. New York: Random House.

Coser, Lewis. 1977. *Masters of Sociological Thought.* New York: Harcourt Brace Jovanovich.

Currie, Elliott, and Jerome H. Skolnick. 1988. *America's Problems: Social Issues and Public Policy.* New York: HarperCollins Publishers.

D'Souza, Dinesh. 1991a. "Illiberal Education." *Atlantic Monthly* (March): 51-79.

D'Souza, Dinesh. 1991b. "In the Name of Academic Freedom, Colleges Should Back Professors Against Students' Demands for 'Correct' Views." *The Chronicles of Higher Education*, 37, (April 24): B1, B3.

DeVault, Marjorie. 1991. *Feeding the Family: The Social Organization of Caring as Gendered Work.* Chicago: University of Chicago Press.

Ehrenreich, Barbara. 1990. "A Conservative Tax Proposal." *Time*, (August): 70.

Eitzen, D. Stanley, and Maxine Baca Zinn. 1992. *In Conflict and Order: Understanding Society.* 5th edition, Boston: Allyn and Bacon.

Eshleman, J. Ross, Barbara G. Cashion, and Laurence A. Basirico. 1993. *Sociology: An Introduction.* 4th edition New York: HarperCollins Publishers.

Eve, Raymond A. and Francis B. Harrold. 1991. *The Creationist Movement in Modern America.* Boston: Twayne.

Frankfort-Nachmias, Chava and David Nachmias. 1992. *Research Methods in the Social Sciences.* 4th edition. New York: St. Martin's Press.

Gergen, Kenneth J. 1991. *The Saturated Self: Dilemmas of Identity in Contemporary Life.* New York: Basic Books.

Gerson, Kathleen. 1992. "Families and Change: Where We Stand and What We Need to Know." *Contemporary Sociology* 21 (July): 444-45.

Gerstel, Naomi. 1992. "Family Nostalgia.." *Contemporary Sociology*, 21 (July): 442-43.

Giddens, Anthony. 1991. *Introduction to Sociology.* New York: W. W. Norton and Company.

Goffman, Erving. 1959. *The Presentation of Self in Everyday Life.* Garden City, New York: Doubleday/Anchor.

Goffman, Erving. 1979. *Gender Advertisements.* Cambridge, Massachusetts: Harvard University Press.

Goldscheider, Frances K., and Linda J. Waite. 1991. *New Families, No Families? The Transformation of the American Home.* Berkeley: University of California Press.

162

Gouldner, Alvin. 1962. "Anti-Minotaur: The Myth of a Value-Free Sociology." (Society for the Study of Social Problems, Presidential Address). *Social Problems* 9 (Winter): 199-213.

Hakuta, Kenji. 1986. *Mirror of Language: The Debate on Bilingualism.* New York: Basic Books.

Hall, Richard H. 1987. *Organizations: Structures, Processes, and Outcomes.* 4th edition. Englewood Cliffs, New Jersey: Prentice Hall.

Haney, C., Banks, W. C., and Zimbardo, P. 1973. "Interpersonal Dynamics in a Simulated Prison." *International Journal of Criminology and Penology* 1: 69-97. (This is more commonly referred to as Zimbardo's study.)

Harris, Chauncy, and Edward L. Ullman. 1945. "The Nature of Cities." *Annals of the American Academy of Political and Social Science*, 242, (November): 7-17.

Haugen, Einar. 1987. *Blessings of Babel: Bilingualism and Language Planning.* Berlin: Mouton de Gruyter.

Henry, William A. 1990. "Beyond the Melting Pot." *Time,* (April 9): 28.

Hess, Beth B., Elizabeth W. Markson, and Peter J. Stein. 1991. *Sociology.* 4th edition. New York: Macmillan Publishing Company.

Hewitt, John. P. 1988. *Self and Society: A Symbolic Interactionist Social Psychology.* 4th edition. Boston: Allyn and Bacon, Inc.

Hoyt, Homer. 1939. *The Structure of Residential Neighborhoods in American Cities.* Washington, D.C.: Federal Housing Administration.

Humphreys, Laud. 1970. *Tearoom Trade: Impersonal Sex in Public Places.* Chicago: Aldine.

Jelen, Ted G. 1991. *The Political Mobilization of Religious Beliefs.* New York: Praeger.

Kagan, Sharon Lynn and James W. Newton. 1989. "For-Profit and Nonprofit Child Care: Similarities and Differences." *Young Children* (November): 4-10.

Kanter, Rosabeth Moss. 1983. *The Change Masters.* New York: Simon and Schuster.

Kart, Cary. 1981. *The Realities of Aging: An Introduction to Gerontology.* Boston: Allyn and Bacon.

Kennedy, Robert E. 1986. *Life Chances: Applying Sociology.* New York: Holt, Rinehart and Winston.

Kinsley, Michael. 1990. "Stat Wars." *The New Republic* (March): 4).

Kontos, Susan. 1990. "For-Profit Programs in the Child Care Delivery System: Bane or Benefit?." *Child and Youth Care Quarterly* 19 (Winter): 211-13.

163

Leavitt, Robin Lynn and Martha Bauman Power. 1989. "Emotional Socialization in the Postmodern Era: Children in Day Care." *Social Psychology Quarterly* 52 (1989): 35-43.

Macoby, Eleanor, and Carol N. Jacklin. 1974. *The Psychology of Sex Differences.* Stanford, California: Stanford University Press.

Magner, Denise. 1991. "Piercing the 'Posturing and Taboo' of Debate on Campus Reforms," *The Chronicles of Higher Education*, 37, (April 10): A3.

Maxwell, Nan L. 1990. *Income Inequality in the United States: 1947-1985.* New York: Greenwood Press

McIntyre, Robert S., Douglas P. Kelly, Michael P. Ettlinger, and Elizabeth A. Fray. 1991. *A Far Cry From Fair: CTJ's Guide to State Tax Reform.* Washington, D. C.: Citizens for Tax Justice.

Milgram, Stanley. 1963. "Behavioral Study of Obedience." Journal of Abnormal and Social Psychology, 67: 371-78.

Neubeck, Kenneth J. 1991. *Social Problems: A Critical Approach*, 3rd ed., New York: McGraw-Hill.

Nielson, Joyce McCarl. 1990. *Sex and Gender in Society: Perspectives on Stratification.* 2d edition. Prospect Heights, Illinois: Waveland Press.

Palmore, Erdman. 1977. "Facts on Aging." *Gerontologist*, 17: 315-20.

Parillo, Vincent N., John Stimson, and Ardyth Stimson. 1989. *Contemporary Social Problems.* 2d edition. New York: Macmillan.

Perrow, Charles. 1986. *Complex Organizations: A Critical Essay.* New York: Random House.

Peters, John F. and Robert H. Waterman. 1982. *In Search of Excellence.* New York: Harper and Row.

Phillips, Deborah, Kathleen McCartney, and Sandra Scarr. 1987. "Child-Care Quality and Children's Social Development. *Developmental Psychology* 23 (1987): 537-543.

Reich, Robert B. 1992 "Whether it's made in America Doesn't Matter in the Global 90s." *Greensboro News and Record*, (Sunday, January 12): B1.

Reich, Robert B. 1991. "Secession of the Successful." *New York Times Magazine*, (March 17): 16-45.

Reich, Robert B. 1991. *The Work of Nations: Preparing Ourselves for 21st-Century Capitalism.* New York: Knopf.

Reiss, Albert. 1968. "Police Brutality: Answers to Key Questions." *Transaction*, 5: 10-19.

164

Ritzer, George. 1988. *Sociological Theory.* 2d edition. New York: Alfred A. Knopf.

Romaine, Suzanne. 1989. *Bilingualism.* Oxford: England: Bail Blackwell.

Rossi, Peter. 1989. *Without Shelter: Homelessness in the 1980s.* New York: Priority Press.

Rossi, Peter. 1989. *Down and Out in America: The Origins of Homelessness in America.* Chicago: University of Chicago Press.

Rothenberg, Paula. 1991. "Critics of Attempts to Democratize the Curriculum Are Waging a Campaign to Misrepresent the Work of Responsible Professors." *The Chronicles of Higher Education,* 37 (April 10): B1, B3.

Sadker, Myra, and David Sadker. 1986. "Sexism in the Classroom: From Grade School to Graduate School." *Phi Delta Kappan* (March): 512-15.

Sadker, Myra, and David Sadker. 1985. "Sexism in the Schoolroom of the '80s." *Psychology Today,* (March): 54-7.

Schutt, Russell K. 1990. "The Quantity and Quality of Homelessness: Research Results and Policy Implications." *Sociological Practice Review,* 1 (August): 77-87.

Serbin, L., and K. O'Leary. 1975. "How Nursery Schools Teach Girls to Shut Up." *Psychology Today* (December): 56-8.

Siegel, Charles N. 1990. "The Brave New World of Children." *New Perspectives Quarterly* 7, (Winter): 34-5.

Singleton, Royce Jr., Bruce C. Straits, Margaret M. Straits, and Ronald J. McAllister. 1988. *Approaches to Social Research.* New York: Oxford University Press.

Skolnick, Arlene. 1992. *The Intimate Environment: Exploring Marriage and the Family.* 5th edition, New York: HarperCollins Publishers.

Skolnick, Arlene. 1991. *Embattled Paradise: The American Family in an Age of Uncertainty.* New York: Basic Books.

Smith, Herman W. 1991. *Strategeis of Social Research.* 3d edition. Orlando, Florida: Holt, Rhinehart and Winston, Inc.

Statistical Abstract (see U.S. Bureau of the Census, *Statistical Abstract of the United States.*

Stoller, P. "The Language Planning Activities of the U.S. Office of Bilingual Education." *International Journal of the Sociology of Language,* 11: 45-60.

Straus, Roger A., ed. 1985. *Using Sociology: An Introduction From the Clinical Perspective.* Bayside, New York: General Hall.

Thio, Alex. 1992. *Sociology: An Introduction.* 3rd edition, New York: HarperCollins Publishers.

Tonnies, Ferdinand. 1963 (originally published in 1887). *Community and Society*. C.P. Loomis, trans., New York: Harper and Row.

Turner, Jonathan H. 1982. *The Structure of Sociological Theory*. Homewood, Illinois: The Dorsey Press.

United Way of America. 1992. *What Lies Ahead: A Decade of Decision*. Alexandria, Virginia: United Way Strategic Institute.

U.S. Bureau of the Census. 1991. *Statistical Abstract of the United States: 1991*. 111th edition. Washington, D.C.: U.S. Government Printing Office.

Waxman, Chaim I. 1983. *The Stigma of Poverty: A Critique of Poverty Theories and Policies*. 2d edition. New York: Pergamon Press.

Weinberger, Caspar. 1990. "The State of the Nation's Schools." *Forbes*, (July 23): 27.

Whitebook, M., C. Howes, and D. Phillips. 1989. *Who Cares? Child Care Teachers and the Quality of Care in America*. Oakland, California: Child Care Employee Project.

Whyte, William Foote. 1949. *Human Relations in the Restaurant Industry*. New York: McGraw-Hill.

Wright, James D. 1989. "Address Unknown: Homelessness in Contemporary America." *Society*, 26 (September/October): 45-53.

Wuthnow, Robert. 1989. *The Struggle for America's Soul: Evangelicals, Liberals, and Secularism*. Grand Rapids, Michigan: William B. Erdmans.